Praise for
Nipped in the Bud, Not in the Butt. How to
Mediation to Resolve Conflicts over Animals

I love the commonsense, practical approach to solving disputes in *Nipped in the Bud, Not in the Butt: How to Use Mediation to Resolve Conflicts over Animals*. The world would be a better place if a sensible mediation approach were used to solve problems.

> – Temple Grandin, Author
> *Animals in Translation*
> *Animals Make Us Human*

During her initial training with my partner Gary Friedman and me at The Center for Understanding in Conflict & The Center for Mediation in Law in 2011, Debra spoke about exploring the application of mediation to conflicts over animals. I have watched Debra grow as a mediator and conflict coach, skillfully handling matters pertaining to disagreements and misunderstandings between people over animals. With Debra's new book, *Nipped in the Bud—Not in the Butt: How to Use Mediation in Conflicts over Animals*, I know more people will choose her methodology to resolve these emotional conflicts involving their beloved animals. It provides a more compassionate way to address, understand, and appreciate everyone's positions and underlying goals so that solutions, in the best interests of all, will be attained. I applaud Debra for her commitment and dedication to this focused area of conflict resolution and for applying the tenets of the Understanding-Based Model of Mediation to these conflicts.

> – Jack Himmelstein, Cofounder
> The Center for Understanding in Conflict
> The Center for Mediation in Law
> **understandinginconflict.org**

Nipped in the Bud, Not in the Butt

How to Use Mediation to Resolve Conflicts over Animals

Debra Vey Voda-Hamilton

ISBN-13: 978-1515020240
ISBN-10: 151502024X
Library of Congress Control Number: 2015911480

CreateSpace Independent Publishing Platform,
   North Charleston, SC

Editorial production:
   Paula L. Fleming and Doug McNair, Fleming Editorial Services
   flemingeditorial.com

Cover and page design:
   Nat Case, INCase, LLC
   incasellc.com

To order or to inquire about special discounts on quantity pur-
   chases, contact the author at **hamiltonlawandmediation.com**.

To Jim, Drew, & Thomas—
Truly the wind beneath my wings in this second chapter.

CONTENTS

Foreword...i

Preface..ix

Section One – Mediation: Nuts and Bolts.................................1

  1. What Is Mediation?..3

    An Example from the Wild West 3

    The History of Mediation 6

    The Function of the Mediator 11

    Mediation Strategies...12

    How Long Does Mediation Take? 14

    How Much Does Mediation Cost? 15

    What Is the Result of Mediation? 17

  2. Why Should I Choose Mediation? 21

    The Importance of Addressing the Conflict...................22

    How People Avoid Addressing the Conflict 24

    Why Not Litigation?...29

    Why Mediation?...31

    The Goals of Mediation: AKA²—

      Address, Keep, Acknowledge & Appreciate 35

    Putting It All Together 42

  3. Mediation Works!...45

    Travis v. Murray 46

    Mediation Is Not Negotiation

      (No Matter What Your Lawyer Says) 51

    Mediation Is About Saving and Keeping Relationships.......53

    Mediation Gets Results 55

  Self-Assessment 1: A Meditation on Mediation........................63

Section Two – How Mediation Works..............................65
   Debra's 6 Tactics for Conflict Mediation 67
   4. Tactic 1: STOP 69
      What Does STOP Mean?..69
      How Do I STOP Talking and Listen? 71
   5. Tactic 2: DROP 75
      What Does DROP Mean?..75
      How Do I DROP the Need to Be Right? 77
   6. Tactic 3: ROLL 81
      What Does ROLL Mean?...81
      How Do I Let What the Other Party Says
        ROLL off My Back?...82
   7. Tactic 4: ADDRESS 85
      What Does ADDRESS Mean?....................................85
      How Do I ADDRESS the Conflict? 85
      Questions for a Positive Discussion 91
   8. Tactic 5: KEEP 95
      What Does KEEP Mean?...95
      How Do I KEEP the Relationship? 95
   9. Tactic 6: ACKNOWLEDGE and APPRECIATE....................99
      What Do ACKNOWLEDGE and
        APPRECIATE Mean?...99
      How Do I ACKNOWLEDGE and APPRECIATE?...........100
   10. Putting It All Together..105
   Self-Assessment 2: A Meditation on Mediation....................107
Section Three – Get Started 109
   11. How to Choose a Mediator or Conflict Coach 111
      Web Searches 112
      Civil Courts and Mediation Centers 113
      Law School Alternative Dispute Resolution
        (ADR) Programs...114
      Other Professional Associations and
        Nonprofit Organizations 115
Conclusion 117
About the Author..121

FOREWORD

In the early 1960s, when I was a college student, I witnessed an incident that left a mark on my consciousness and has continued to serve as a source of reflection. I saw a neighbor of mine, wearing only a bathrobe, running down the street with a dead dog in her arms. The woman was crying bitterly, even hysterically, and shouting "First my mother dies, and now you." She was inconsolable, and it was of no help at all to her when neighbors attempted to provide comfort by pointing out "It's only a dog—you can get another one."

Within a decade, no one possessed of any sensitivity would so deride expressions of grief at the loss of a beloved pet. By the late 1970s, the Colorado State University veterinary school, where I taught, employed a staff of grief counselors to help distraught clients. On one occasion, a group of tough motorcyclists riding Harley-Davidsons brought a sick Chihuahua to our veterinary hospital. The dog was intractably ill and required euthanasia to prevent further suffering. So distraught were the bikers that the grief counselors felt compelled to find them a motel room because the staff did not believe they could ride safely.

A similar state of affairs was widely noted during disasters such as Hurricane Katrina in 2005, when people refused to be evacuated from flooded areas without their pets, risking injury and even death. Eventually, authorities acquiesced to the strength of this bond and adopted a policy of evacuating companion animals along with their owners. Clearly, people are willing to display a powerful bond with their companion animals that a few short years ago would have been socially unacceptable. To what can we attribute this attitudinal change?

It is clear that the dog has played a unique and important role in the development of humans, having been with us since the birth of humanity. (Recent evidence in China indicates that tame wolves were associated with Peking Man about five hundred thousand years ago.) The dog evidences in countless ways its fulfillment of the contract with humans. The dog has been, and still is, a guardian of the home, a warrior and messenger, a sentry, a playmate for and protector of children, a guardian of sheep and cattle, a beast of burden, a rescuer of lost people, a puller of carts and sleds, a friend, a hunter, a companion, a constant assistant to people who are deaf or blind or have other disabilities, and an exercise mate. And humans have shaped the dog to have all sorts of physical forms and personalities such that the domestic dog is literally incapable of survival outside of human society. (Consider the bulldog, or the Chihuahua.) According to some ethologists, notably Konrad Lorenz, humans have actually developed the dog into a creature whose natural pack structure has been integrated into human society, with the human master playing the traditional role of pack leader. It is hard to imagine a more vivid and pervasive example of a social contract, an agreement in nature and action, than that obtaining between humans and dogs.

Let us look for a moment at some of the more surprising ways that the dog is integral to human life. These animals are viewed as members of the family, as friends—as "givers and receivers of love" as one judge put it. The bond based in pragmatic symbiosis has turned into a bond based in love. A love-based bond imposes a higher and more stringent set of moral obligations than does one based solely in mutual pragmatic benefit.

The rise of deep, love-based relationships with animals as a regular and increasingly accepted social phenomenon arose from a variety of converging and mutually reinforcing social conditions. In the first place, probably beginning with the widespread use of the automobile, extended nuclear families with multiple generations living in one location or under one roof began to vanish. At the beginning of the twentieth century, when roughly half of the public was employed in agriculture, significant numbers of large extended families lived together on farms. The safety net for older people was their family, rather than society as a whole. Subsequently, however, easy mobility made preserving the extended family less necessary. At the same time, people began to view society as a whole, rather than the family unit, as responsible for assuring a secure retirement, medical attention, and a safe living situation for elderly people.

The tendency of urban life to erode community, to create what the Germans called *Gesellshaft* rather than *Gemeinschaft*—mixtures rather than compounds as it were—further engendered solitude and loneliness as modes of being. Correlatively, selfishness and self-actualization were established as positive values beginning in the highly individualistic 1960s. The divorce rate began to climb, and the traditional stigma attached to divorce was erased. Also, as medical advances prolonged our life spans, more and more people outlived their working years and experienced disability and accompanying loneliness, and the loss of the extended family removed a possible remedy.

In effect, we have lonely old people, lonely divorced people, and, most tragically, lonely children whose single parent often works. With the best jobs being urban, or quasi-urban, many people live in cities or suburbs. In New York City, for example, where I lived for twenty-six years, one can be lonelier than in rural Wyoming. The cowboy craving camaraderie can find a neighbor from whom he is separated only by physical distance; the urban person may know no one and have no one in reach who cares. Shorn of physical space, people create psychic distance between themselves and others. People may (and usually do) live for years six inches away from neighbors in apartment buildings and never exchange a sentence. Watch New Yorkers on an elevator; the rule is to stand as far away from others as you can and study the ceiling. Making eye contact on the street can be taken as a challenge or a sexual invitation, so people avoid eye contact. One steps over and around drunks on the street. One minds one's own business. "Don't get involved" is a mantra for survival.

Yet humans need love, companionship, and emotional support. We need to be needed. In such a world, a companion animal can be one's psychic and spiritual salvation. Divorce lawyers repeatedly tell me that custody of the dog can be a greater source of conflict than is custody of the children! An animal is someone to hug and hug you back—someone to play with, to laugh with, to take a walk with, to share beautiful days with, to cry with. For a child, the dog is a playmate, a friend, someone to talk to. The dog is a protector: one of the most unforgettable photos I have ever seen shows a child of six in an apartment answering the door at night while clutching the collar of a 200-pound Great Dane, protected.

But a dog is more than that. In New York and other big, cold, tough cities, it is a social lubricant. One does not talk to strangers in cities, unless he or she—or preferably both of you—are walking a dog. Then the barriers crumble. One of the most extraordinary social phenomena I have ever participated in was the "dog people" in the Upper West Side of Manhattan. These were people who walked their dogs at roughly the same time—morning and evening—in Riverside Park. Among these people who were united by a common and legitimate purpose, having dogs in common and thereby being above each other's suspicion, conversations would begin spontaneously. To be sure, we usually did not know each other's names—we were "Red's owner," "Helga's person," "Fluffy's mistress." But names didn't matter. What mattered was we began to care for each other through the magic of sharing a bond with an animal and the animals' not knowing New York etiquette and playing with one another and our caring for each other's animals.

For more old people than I care to recall, the dog (or cat) was a reason to get up in the morning, to go out, to bundle up and go to the park ("Fluffy misses her friends, you know!"), to shop, to fuss, to feel responsible for a life, and to feel needed.

I used to walk my Great Dane very late at night, feeling safe, and other people would speak to me. Once I encountered a black woman who had gotten off at the wrong subway station while heading for Harlem and was terrified. With no hesitation, she asked me to walk her a mile to Harlem, where she felt safe. "I'm okay with you and that big dog," she said, never even imagining that I could be a monster with a dog!

Most memorably, I recall walking miles to the theater district at 4:00 a.m. At one all-night cafeteria, the prostitutes used to assemble after a night's work. "Helga!" they would shout with delight when my dog approached. I was simply attached to the leash and was addressed only when they asked permission to buy her a doughnut. These guarded, cynical women would get on their knees and hug and kiss the dog, with a genuine warmth and pleasure, letting the child in them show through in these rare and priceless moments. I cannot recall these incidents without emotion.

Our companion animals, in today's world, provide us with love and someone to love, and they do so unfailingly, with loyalty, grace, and boundless devotion.

Our pets have become sources of friendship and company for the old and the lonely, vehicles for penetrating the frightful shell surrounding a disturbed child, beings that provide the comfort of touch to even the most asocial person, and inexhaustible sources of pure, unqualified love.

Small wonder, then, that it is not uncommon for significant feuding to occur between neighbors over the behavior of a dog. The dog barks too late at night, the dog defecates on the neighbor's lawn, the dog frightens children in the neighborhood, the dog has treed someone's cat, or the dog is of a certain breed around which ubiquitous but hyperbolic urban legends about viciousness and aggression have developed. The neighbor calls the police or chases or threatens the dog, and thus begins a conflict that can endure for years.

Obviously, one of the regular vehicles for resolving such conflict is the legal system. In most cases, however, this is not a satisfactory solution. Decisions emerging from law display no sensitivity to the parties involved. Many of us have lived through such disputes, and their punitive legal resolution tends to leave the parties involved harboring a great deal of resentment toward those whom they feel created the conflict. This may result in such unsatisfactory "resolutions" as neighbors pointedly and deliberately ignoring each other, paranoid fantasies that the neighbor will harm the animal, and even physically violent altercations.

Litigation resolves disagreement with little concern for battlefield casualties. The pain of conflict remains. Whether you win or lose, the bad relationship with a neighbor continues to be a pebble in your shoe. You cannot encounter the neighbor without an immense feeling of awkwardness. You find yourself peeping out of the window to avoid any need for interaction. Your home, which should be your castle as the cliché goes, now becomes a source of stress. You worry about the picture of you that the neighbor is painting to other neighbors. You worry about the neighbor harboring ill will toward you and evil awaiting the opportunity to strike back. You worry, based on urban legends you have heard, about the neighbor poisoning your dog. Even if you have won through litigation, there may well be a strong feeling that you have lost. The situation is more than a little like being sued. No one wins; factions are created; your entire mode of living is altered in an uncomfortable way.

One solution to this sort of aggravated problem has tended to escape the notice of parties in conflict: sympathetic, perceptive, and wise mediation. Mediation is significantly different. If one is fortunate enough to find a wise and compassionate third-party mediator like Debra Hamilton, the result is not only a bandage over a wound but genuine healing that does not leave a scar. To be sure, mediation requires that both parties be people of goodwill, whose ego does not interfere with their decency. It creates a situation where both parties can move on and ideally, at some future time, even laugh at themselves and perhaps be friends. (Abraham Lincoln once remarked that the best way to vanquish an enemy is to make him a friend.) Mediation depends on Plato's insight that far and away the best society is one that has within it good people; good laws represent a poor second. Ms. Hamilton has been a litigator and clearly understands the inherent superiority of mediation. This is a wise, superb, and moral book that I can unequivocally recommend to all confronting conflict over animals.

> Bernard E. Rollin, University Distinguished Professor
> Department of Philosophy,
> Colorado State University
> Professor of Philosophy, Animal Sciences, and
> Biomedical Sciences and University Bioethicist

PREFACE

If you go on enough road trips, you'll eventually spot a certain memorable bumper sticker. It's very politically incorrect, and it goes like this:

My wife, definitely.
My dog … maybe.
My gun, never!

It's sexist and just plain rude, but it illustrates a common misconception that brings a lot of people to me for help. I'm a lawyer who works with people who are in disputes over animals. Many of my clients are parties in a divorce, and while they are always hurt and angry, they are usually able to think rationally enough about the situation to reach an out-of-court settlement and divide up their marital property without resorting to costly litigation. This is to everyone's benefit, so it's the approach most divorce attorneys recommend and most divorcing couples take … right up until someone asks, "What about the dog?" Then all hell breaks loose, and the settlement goes right out the window.

This is something I've learned through many years of experience. I was a litigator for 30 years, and early in my career, I never thought to start off a divorce settlement negotiation by asking my client, "Do you have a pet?" After all, why would I? If I were working up a settlement offer and someone on my staff had raised a red flag that my client and his spouse had a dog, I would have thought, *Really, are you kidding? It's a dog! That's going to break up this agreement?* Well, as I found out, it did—a lot. In fact, any settlement will likely fall apart if the divorcing parties do not give top priority to deciding how they will share ownership of and responsibility for their beloved pet after their divorce.

Our attachment to the animals we love is primal, and it goes deeper than we can ever understand. Early humans domesticated animals as

> *Our attachment to the animals we love is primal, and it goes deeper than we can ever understand.*

a matter of survival, and a recent theory proposed by anthropologist Dr. Pat Shipman holds that early humans who domesticated dogs were more likely to survive than those who didn't. This was due to the fact that humans and dogs could hunt together to bring down more and larger prey in times of food scarcity, like during the last Ice Age. Dr. Shipman also asserts that this early human-canine bond led to the extinction of the Neanderthals, who competed with our ancestors for food and territory but who did not domesticate and hunt with dogs. This was a disadvantage that would eventually prove fatal.[1] Therefore, early humans who formed the strongest attachments to their animals were more likely to beat out their competitors and survive. That means our powerful love of animals is part of our genetic heritage, and it's one of the reasons we see red when one of our animals becomes the object of a dispute.

So to whoever wrote that bumper sticker, I'd like to just say this: You're wrong. We love our animals more than our property and most of the people in our lives, and our strong desire to keep and defend our animals is one of our most basic survival mechanisms. That goes far deeper than our political opinions, so realistically, your bumper sticker should say this:

> *My spouse, definitely.*
> *My gun ... talk to my lawyer.*
> *My dog, never!*

That's how we really feel about our animals. Disputes over animals are some of the most emotional conflicts in existence, and that's why they're so difficult to resolve. People either avoid addressing disputes over animals to avoid dealing with the volatile emotions involved, or they go straight to litigation, where our legal system doesn't take into account the emotional needs of the disputing parties or even the welfare of the animal. The law treats our pets as property—just things—and any judge will be bound by whatever the statutes say about property when making a decision about an animal at the center of a dispute. The court will award ownership of the animal or decide the animal's fate based on the law, not based on what may be best for the animal and the people who love the animal. That's why going to litigation first to resolve a dispute over an animal is always a losing proposition.

But there's a better way—mediation. Mediation happens outside a courtroom, in a setting where property law does not come into play. In mediation, the disputing parties come together with a neutral mediator so they can hear each other out, acknowledge each other's emotions and points of view, and re-

> *I am passionate about helping people resolve disagreements and misunderstandings that involve the animals they so dearly love.*

solve their dispute in a way that satisfies their emotional needs while putting the welfare of the animal first. Mediation is the best way to resolve disputes over animals, protect those animals, and repair the human relationships that are at the core of such disputes.

And that's why I wrote this book. I am passionate about helping people resolve disagreements and misunderstandings that involve the animals they so dearly love. When I was a trial lawyer, I repeatedly witnessed battles between parties who would get so wrapped up in the law that they would lose sight of what was best for everyone, especially the animal. Relationships were destroyed as attorneys, having no emotional attachment to the issues, would argue the case based solely on the letter of the law.

My final case exemplified why I needed to change my perspective and fight for the animals. I represented a family who was being sued by a rescue organization. Try as I might, the pro bono attorney representing the rescue organization would never speak with me. I ultimately won the case, but only after my client spent thousands of dollars to defend themselves for taking actions that were in the best interest of the dog. The plaintiff's attorney simply wanted to enforce a contract, and the rescue organization chose to fight because they were angry—totally ignoring the welfare of the dog, the good intentions of the owners, and what was really best for themselves. It was a senseless battle, so after it was done, I hung up my litigation pumps forever.

Now I mediate interpersonal conflicts that involve animals. It is amazing how often these conflicts occur and how much animosity they generate. There are no winners in such conflicts if they remain unaddressed or go to litigation. That's why in this book, I explain how mediation can help you resolve such conflicts peacefully and to the benefit of you and all other parties, especially your animals. I hope that through this book, I can provide you with lessons that will help you resolve such conflicts in ways that ensure that the needs of your animals and their caregivers are respected, understood, and fulfilled.

---

1. Pat Shipman, *The Invaders: How Humans and Their Dogs Drove Neanderthals to Extinction* (Cambridge, MA: The Belknap Press of Harvard University Press, 2015).

Section One
MEDIATION: NUTS AND BOLTS

Discourage litigation. Persuade your neighbors to compromise whenever you can. Point out to them how the nominal winner is often a real loser—in fees, expenses, and waste of time. As a peacemaker the lawyer has a superior opportunity of being a good man. There will still be business enough.

—Abraham Lincoln[1]

Even though mediation has a long and successful history in the United States and around the world, it is often misunderstood. Sometimes people who would benefit from mediation avoid it because they think it's too expensive or won't get results. Sometimes ostensible "mediators" don't actually practice mediation. When done right, mediation is a cost-effective way of getting better results than can be achieved by avoiding the problem, retaliating personally, or suing in court.

---

1. Abraham Lincoln, Notes for a law lecture, c. July 1, 1850,
   www.abrahamlincolnonline.org/lincoln/speeches/lawlect.htm.

Chapter 1
WHAT IS MEDIATION?

We can work it out. Life is very short, and there's no time for fussing and fighting, my friend.

—John Lennon and Paul McCartney [1]

In mediation, a neutral party helps two or more disputing parties confidentially address and resolve their dispute to their mutual satisfaction. The mediator does not make a decision or suggest a solution to the conflict, as would an arbitrator, nor does the mediator impose a ruling upon the parties based on the law, as would a judge. Instead, a mediator facilitates agreement between disputing parties, using specialized skills to help the parties come together, address their conflict, communicate their feelings and points of view, listen to each other respectfully, and ultimately resolve the conflict between themselves. Only the disputing parties know what the best resolution to their own conflict is, but they can't reach that resolution in a mutually acceptable way—one that satisfies their deeper emotional needs—without the right skills to do so. A mediator provides those skills and takes the parties through a time-tested process to help them resolve their dispute.

AN EXAMPLE FROM THE WILD WEST

Cast your mind back to a time when people living on the American frontier didn't always have lawmen to protect them or judges to help them settle disputes. Families often settled their differences among themselves, on their own terms. Say that in the late 1700s, two families—the Logans and the Joneses—settled on land near each other. Initially, they got along fine, but then a Logan man stole a hog from a Jones woman. Words were exchanged, and then blows, and then someone was shot. Soon, both families were in an uproar, and the conflict turned into an open feud.

This is based on a true story! The theft of a single hog started the famous feud between the Hatfields and the McCoys.[2] Since those two families didn't have a mediator to help them resolve their conflict, their feud went on for over a century, resulting in many deaths and a legal case that went all the way to the US Supreme Court. Hopefully things will turn out differently for our Logans and Joneses.

> *The feud between the Hatfields and McCoys went on for over a century, with many deaths and a legal case that went all the way to the US Supreme Court.*

It's now the mid-1800s. The people who started the feud are long gone, and in fact, neither family knows what started it. Everyone just tells stories about all the horrible things the other family has done down through the years, stories that get worse in the retelling. The families never talk to each other, so there's no way they can address the conflict. It also doesn't matter that there are lawmen and courts in the area now. If the sheriff arrests a Jones who tries to hurt a Logan (or vice versa), the feud just goes on because the families still want revenge. The law can't help people deal with their emotions in a way that will allow them to call a truce and start listening to each other.

Then one day, an old man comes riding down out of the mountains. Jeremiah has got to be pushing 80, but he's still just as vital as he was 60 years ago, when he guided the first Logans and Joneses westward to these lands. Both families welcome him into their homes, and they tell him about the feud that's been going on since before they were born. He asks them how it started, and each family tells him all their terrible stories about the other family.

Jeremiah is grieved to hear how badly the two families have fallen out. He knew the Logans and the Joneses back in the old days, and many of them liked and even loved each other. If both families could just start talking to each other again, perhaps they could resolve their differences. He offers to arrange a meeting between the two families so he can help them put an end to all this.

After a lot of grumbling, the Logans and the Joneses agree to meet, but only out of respect for Jeremiah. They know the old man's not on anyone's side—he's just a friend of both families who wants to see the fighting stop. At the meeting, Jeremiah invites the elders of both families to stand up, tell their stories, and vent their emotions. He keeps the peace, telling them to listen to each other. As the stories come out, there's both shock and laughter as each family points out the flaws in the other family's stories. Jim hadn't been born yet, Belle had gotten married and moved away, and Billy-Bob was already in jail when they say he killed Old Joe. The only things that check out as true are the theft of the hog, the bad feelings it caused, and all the fighting and murders that followed. Slowly, both families realize that all their lives, they've really been feuding over the theft of one hog—an event that created bad feelings way out of proportion to the harm done.

They decide that the violence doesn't make sense and must stop, but they're still not sure how to do this. After all, there are still wrongs that must be righted. Jeremiah doesn't tell them how. Instead, he asks them what it would take to satisfy their emotional needs so they can let the feud go. Over the rest of the evening, the two families propose solutions to each other until they find one they can agree on. Finally, the elders of both families stand up and apologize to each other for the long years of bloodshed, the Logans ceremonially return a new hog to the Joneses, and everyone shakes hands and promise to live in peace.

In this story, the old man was the mediator, and the process he took the two families through was mediation. Jeremiah was a neutral third party whose only goal was to help the Logans and the Joneses find the best resolution to their own conflict. He did not suggest a solution, quote the law, or send anyone to jail. Instead, he skillfully helped the feuding families listen to each other and acknowledge what was true about each other's stories. Then he asked each of them what it would take to resolve the conflict. In the end, they resolved their own conflict to their mutual satisfaction.

THE HISTORY OF MEDIATION

Though the story of the Logans and the Joneses is set in early America, the history of mediation goes back much further than that. In fact, mediation is a long-standing tradition in many cultures, and many of these still consider mediation preferable to litigation.

For example, the Chinese philosopher Confucius (551–479 BCE) established that it is best to resolve disputes through moral persuasion and mutual agreement, rather than through coercion. Buddhist traditions hold to the same principle, so as a result, litigation is only used as a last resort in China and other parts of Asia. In fact, modern-day businesses surveyed in the Asia-Pacific region strongly favor using mediation rather than litigation.[3] The government of Japan has even set up procedural barriers to litigation, and as a result, lawyers are few in Japan. On the other hand, there are many mediators there, since mediation has a long history going back to the practice of village elders mediating disputes. Finally, there's simply a social stigma against litigation. People all across Asia view litigation as involving a loss of face—a huge difference in attitude from ours in the litigious United States![4]

In many other non-Western cultures, tribal elders have served as mediators since ancient times, and they often still command more respect than do the courts, judges, and officeholders of the elected government. In the Muslim tradition, for example, mediation is often seen as preferable to litigation because judges may make wrong decisions and because litigation requires disclosing private matters in public.[5]

This has practical consequences. After the fall of Saddam Hussein, the US occupational authorities in Iraq initially tried to negotiate major projects with the newly established Iraqi government—but this didn't work because those negotiations deliberately excluded the Iraqi tribal sheikhs, who had traditionally served as mediators.[6] Things only improved when the occupational authorities started working with the sheikhs. Indeed, a friend of a colleague of mine was a major in the US Army during and after the Iraq War, and he said that it was impossible to get anything done if you didn't understand the dual-track nature of negotiations there. You had to negotiate with the elected and appointed government officials, but you also had to negotiate with the sheikhs. Only if you came to an agreement with the sheikhs about the issue at hand could they then go mediate among all the other people involved (sometimes even the elected officials you had just negotiated with!) so that everyone's differences could be ironed out and the project could move forward. Thus, mediation is a powerful force for getting things done in many parts of the world.

Mediation in the United States

In the United States, mediation has a history going back to colonial times. In 1774, two Quakers named David Barclay and David Fothergill attempted to prevent the outbreak of the Revolutionary War by mediating between Benjamin Franklin and British prime minister Lord North.[7]

Then in the 1800s, mediation became the primary strategy for dealing with the labor unrest that was disrupting many businesses, sometimes resulting in violence. In 1913, the US Department of Labor started appointing professional mediators known as Commissioners of Conciliation. Later, the National Labor Relations Act of 1935 established collective bargaining through mediation as the official method of settling labor-management disputes, and the Labor Department facilitated this process in 1946 by establishing the Federal Mediation and Conciliation Service. This service employed a staff of full-time mediators whose job was to facilitate negotiations between unions and management.

Mediation again took on national importance in the United States during the struggle for civil rights in the 1960s. Widespread civil unrest led the US Department of Justice to create the Community Relations Service, staffing it with mediators whose job was to bring together people who were in conflict over civil rights. Private organizations like the American Arbitration Association also stepped forward to provide mediators for civil rights conflicts.

At the same time, courts overburdened with violent crime cases turned to mediators to help resolve minor offenses and disputes by mediating out-of-court settlements between the parties involved. Many such offenses and disputes were part of ongoing situations in the community, and they were driven by personal or group animosities that would not have been quelled by declaring someone guilty and sending him to jail. Mediators were in a much better position to bring people together, validate their emotions and points of view, and help them find ways to reconcile and make amends for what they'd done.

State and local governments began to institute mediation programs in which law professors and later law students acted as out-of-court mediators. Then in 1977, the US Department of Justice began to create Neighborhood Justice Centers, which served as models for later government-run mediation programs designed to keep minor offenses and civil disputes out of the courts whenever possible. By the end of the 1990s, over half the federal courts had instituted mediation programs to divert cases from the courts as appropriate, and they assigned trained mediators to handle these cases.

Mediation Done Right

Sadly, as Judith A. Saul points out, community mediation didn't always meet with success. This was due to how the courts defined the goals of mediation and what they expected the mediators to do. Essentially, the courts were asking mediators to function in ways that undermined the mediation process:

> Mediators were oriented toward settling cases and, in the process, they often strayed from the idea of party self-determination.
>
> … Most mediators used a staged model, guiding parties through a series of steps that structured how parties talked to each other. While this, in and of itself, had the effect of controlling content, most mediators were more overt in limiting what parties talked about. By being selective rather than inclusive in what they responded to, mediators shaped the conversation in a direction that, in their opinion, increased the chances of solving the problem. They tended to prioritize concrete topics over emotional content. They contained conflict through the use of ground rules and caucuses. Since mediators were actively involved as problem-solvers, they had to understand the situation, so they asked lots of questions, made suggestions, and used their position to influence or persuade the parties. Other mediators … went even farther. In many court-based programs, mediators were expected to have content expertise so that they could evaluate the strength of each side's arguments and predict likely court outcomes. Thus mediators subtly or not-so-subtly offered advice as a way to ensure that any agreement reached met either their own sense of what was right or fair or the court's standards.
>
> The practice of mediation developed in this way because mediators were focused on problem-solving

or transactional bargains. With programs dependent on the courts for cases, their interest in pleasing the courts outweighed their commitment to party control.[8]

The professional mediation community responded to these problems by implementing new and improved mediation techniques, and today, there are several techniques that a skilled mediator can choose from depending on the situation (see "Mediation Strategies" below). The hypothetical example set in the Wild West helps us better understand mediation by demonstrating what it is and is not. A mediator is a neutral party who is committed to helping the disputing parties resolve their conflict in a mutually satisfactory way, and mediation is a process whereby the disputing parties discover their own solution and make their own agreement, which can be kept confidential. The court system, in contrast, sometimes pressured community mediation programs to promote a process in which mediators were not neutral. Instead, they tried to impose what they felt was a reasonable solution on the process based on the courts' priorities, the mediators' own priorities, and the courts' and mediators' ideas of what was best for the disputing parties. Such a process is not mediation, and it is doomed to failure almost every time.

> *A mediator is a neutral party who is committed to helping the disputing parties resolve their conflict in a mutually satisfactory way, and mediation is a process whereby the disputing parties discover their own solution and make their own agreement, which can be kept confidential.*

THE FUNCTION OF THE MEDIATOR

So how does a mediator work her magic? How does she bring parties in conflict together and get them communicating in ways that end up making them want to resolve the situation? Well, a clue to this comes from the wisdom of the ancient Chinese philosopher Lao Tzu:

> The great leader speaks little.
> He never speaks carelessly.
> He works without self-interest
> and leaves no trace.
> When all is finished, the people say,
> "We did it ourselves."[9]

That's the key to good mediation: in the end, the disputing parties must know that they created their own solution among themselves. If a solution is imposed upon them, their need for validation of their emotions, respect for their points of view, and meaningful closure will not be met, and the conflict will either continue or die down for a while but spring up again later. Therefore, a mediator must be that great leader who speaks carefully, listens, and works without self-interest in ways that get people to say they have created their own solution themselves because, in fact, they have.

To achieve this goal, a mediator must wear many hats. Mediate.com lists them as follows:

- Convener
- Educator
- Communication Facilitator
- Translator
- Questioner and Clarifier
- Process Adviser
- Angel of Realities
- Catalyst
- Responsible Detail Person[10]

As you can see, none of these roles involves laying down rules about what must happen or persuading the disputing parties to accept a particular solution. Instead, the mediator brings the disputing parties together, educates them about the mediation process, makes sure they are listening to each other and themselves, advises them as to whether certain options are realistic, suggests new options or perspectives for the purpose of stimulating new conversations, keeps track of all the details, and finally helps the parties write up and implement their own agreement.

MEDIATION STRATEGIES

As mentioned, mediation professionals have developed several mediation models. These give mediators alternative approaches to mediating different types of disputes among clients with differing needs. Some of these models are listed below.

Facilitative mediation. This is the traditional form of mediation, in which a mediator creates a structured process designed to help the disputing parties reach a mutually satisfactory resolution. The mediator's job is to ask questions, validate both parties' feelings and points of view, help the two sides discover their common interests, and assist both parties in evaluating different options for resolution.

Whenever possible, facilitative mediators hold joint sessions with the disputing parties, helping people come to a resolution through hearing each other out and discovering their own solution to the dispute. They will also work with the parties "in caucus," meaning that they speak with each of the parties in separate rooms. The advantage of this approach is that the parties feel they can speak fully to the mediator. However, a disadvantage of the caucus approach is that the mediator has all the information but can't necessarily share it. The caucus approach is not usually as effective as having the parties speak directly to each other.[11]

Understanding-based mediation. In this model, the mediator seeks to resolve conflict through deepening the conflicting parties' understanding of themselves, each other, and conflict itself. The model focuses on helping the parties understand their priorities, perspectives, and concerns and find out what lies underneath their conflict—not just the obvious facts of who did what to whom. It stresses that conflict is fueled by subjective factors like beliefs, assumptions, feelings, the need to assign blame, the need for self-justification, and preconceived ideas about the nature of conflict itself—like ideas about the exclusivity of right and wrong. Ultimately, this model seeks to help people understand that the multilayered nature of conflict puts them in a "conflict trap." Only by understanding the nature of conflict and their own ideas about it can they break out of that trap and resolve their own conflict.[12]

Transformative mediation. This form of mediation differs from the others in that it doesn't focus on resolving the conflict but instead seeks to transform the quality of the interaction between the disputing parties from negative and destructive to positive and constructive. It views conflict not as a clash of power, rights, or interests but as a crisis in human interaction. Saul describes transformative mediation as follows:

> The goals of a transformative mediator are to support party decision-making and inter-party perspective-taking. They reflect the reorientation of the mediator from transaction to interaction, from conflict resolution to conflict transformation.... Transformative mediators attend to the moment-to-moment interaction between the parties[,] not the problem and its potential solution. They follow rather than lead.... They avoid leading because doing so assumes that the mediator, not the parties, knows what is best in a given situation.[13]

Transformative mediators still have a goal of helping parties resolve their dispute. They also believe that transforming the quality of interaction has the best chance of preventing the disputing parties from getting into new conflicts after they've resolved their current conflict.

As you can see, there are many similarities among these three mediation models. They all seek to empower the disputing parties to resolve their own conflict by finding their own best solution. The differences among these models are largely a matter of emphasis. Facilitative mediation emphasizes communication, mutual validation of perspectives and emotions, finding common ground, and reaching a mutually satisfactory solution. Understanding-based mediation emphasizes understanding one's self, each other, and the nature of conflict, thus helping people break out of conflict patterns that keep them at loggerheads. Transformative mediation emphasizes transforming people's negative interactions into positive, constructive ones, with the mediator focusing on keeping moment-to-moment interactions positive. In all three mediation styles, however, the mediator acts as a neutral party, helping to create the conditions that will ultimately result in the parties' reaching a mutually acceptable resolution of their conflict.

HOW LONG DOES MEDIATION TAKE?

Given all the processes described above, how long does mediation usually take? The simple answer is that mediation takes much less time than litigation. While court cases can drag on for months or even years, some mediations are resolved in a day or less. Some might require two sessions, mediations involving complex divorce settlements might take several weeks, and other situations can take longer depending on how long it takes the parties to arrange to meet and other factors. However, the overall message is clear: if you're looking to resolve your conflict as quickly as possible, mediation is the way to go.[14]

HOW MUCH DOES MEDIATION COST?

Once again, the answer is much less than litigation. Professional mediators may bill by the hour or by the session, and more experienced mediators or mediators with expertise in a particular area may charge more than others. Nonetheless, the cost differences between litigation and mediation are startling, for the following reasons:

- In litigation, each party has to hire a lawyer and pay all of that lawyer's fees. In mediation, both parties hire the same mediator and can split the mediator's fees between them.
- Bringing a lawsuit involves paying a court filing fee that can run into hundreds of dollars, and then it involves paying a lawyer to do research and file motions, which can cost hundreds of dollars more. There are no court filing fees in mediation because mediation does not go to court.
- Whenever you talk to your lawyer on the phone, you are paying him his hourly rate, and whenever your lawyer talks to the judge, you are also paying your lawyer his hourly rate. Then there's months of discovery, paying for a court reporter, paying for expert witnesses, and even paying to use the courtroom. The cumulative costs for all this can run into tens or even hundreds of thousands of dollars. With mediation, you are simply paying your mediator's hourly fee, which is usually anywhere from $100 to $300 an hour. Since mediation usually takes just a day or two … do the math and see how much less you'll be paying with mediation than you would in litigation.[15]

So all by themselves, the cost savings of mediation should be enough to steer you away from litigation. But there's more. The emotional nature of disputes over animals can cause hurt feelings to become monetized to the tune of thousands of dollars. If someone's pet has died, for example, that person is grieving deeply. If they blame their veterinarian and the conflict goes to court, that emotional hurt can be assigned dollar signs—big ones. That's why it's crucial to use mediation, which deals with and resolves emotions, and not litigation, which doesn't.

I call this the "How Much Is That Doggie in the Window?" problem. In a divorce, for example, having the dog in the living room window can cost a huge amount of money in legal fees or money left on the table if both parties want to keep the pet outright. The couple acquired the pet in better times, so the pet represents those good times and all the aspirations for the future and commitment to that future together that were part of the relationship back then—and aren't part of the relationship anymore. That's what makes the pet issue so emotional. There are even times when a pet is held hostage in exchange for money. I often ask my divorce attorney colleagues to mediate the discussion over the pet because if they give the parties a confidential opportunity to talk about why the dog is worth $20,000, they'll find out why. The party holding the pet hostage for cash will say to the other party, "You didn't do the laundry, you went out with the dog but not me, you cooked for the dog but not me, and that's why it's going to cost you $20,000 to keep the dog!" Attorneys think people who make these arguments are crazy—but they're not. This pet was part of the fabric of their relationship, and attorneys ignore that fact at their peril. I've had half a dozen attorneys walk up to me and say, "Boy, I wish I had you a month ago, two months ago, ten years ago, because a divorce settlement almost went down the toilet because once we got to the pet, there was no agreement and it became ugly."

> *Only by going through the mediation process will the need to monetize hurt feelings be reduced and hopefully eliminated.*

So due to the emotionally fraught nature of disputes over pets—whether during divorce or any other conflict—it is crucial to go to mediation so the angry parties can talk in a confidential setting and express their emotions over the pet in a way that creates mutual understanding, reducing the need to get their pound of flesh from the other party. Only by going through that emotional process will the need to monetize hurt feelings be reduced and hopefully eliminated.

WHAT IS THE RESULT OF MEDIATION?

With one set of divorcing clients I had, the attorney representing the husband said, "You deserve 50 percent of this pet because you've paid half of this dog's bills." Based on that advice and because he really loved the dog—he loved going out on hikes with the dog, and he loved the dog being home when he got there—the husband fought hammer and tongs for 50 percent of this dog. However, no one had ever discussed with him the reality of having the dog live with him when he lived alone and worked full-time. In our mediation, which took about 8 hours, we did a lot of reality checking about what part of the dog each party wanted. In the end, they decided that the dog would live with the ex-wife most of the time. When she went on vacation, however, the ex-husband would get the dog, and he would also get the dog one weekend a month so the two could go for walks in the mountains together and generally hang out.

He said, "You know, this is what I love about my pet." He was a teacher and was in school all day, so how was he going to take care of a pet every day? It just wasn't going to happen. Because of the agreement that he and his ex-wife reached through mediation, he's now able to spend time with his dog the one weekend a month when he's not busy, thereby keeping the dog in his life.

And the best part? The divorced parties worked out a way to transfer the dog between them. Through mediation, they worked out an agreement where the dog is dropped off at a doggy daycare by one person and then picked up by the other person later. The two parties never have to see each other, but the dog gets the benefit of being with both his family members. Before they went to mediation, this ex-couple couldn't come up with this creative solution because they were so angry with each other over the divorce.

This dog has lived a wonderful life, and his owners have both been able to keep him in their lives. It's a win-win for everyone—especially the dog. That's what mediation provides.

> *It's a win-win for everyone— especially the dog.*

1. John Lennon and Paul McCartney, "We Can Work It Out," released December 1965, Capitol Records (US), double A-side single with "Day Tripper."

2. "The Hatfield & McCoy Feud," History.com, accessed May 14, 2015, **www.history.com/shows/hatfields-and-mccoys/articles/the-hatfield-mccoy-feud/.**

3. International Institute for Conflict Prevention and Resolution, "Attitudes Toward ADR in the Asia-Pacific Region: A CPR Survey," 2013, **www.cpradr.org/Portals/0/Asia-Pacific%20Survey.pdf.**

4. Mediation Matters, "History of Mediation," 2011, accessed May 14, 2015, **www.mediationmatterssd.com/mediationmatters/history.html**.

5. Pew Research Center, "Applying God's Law: Religious Courts and Mediation in the U.S.," April 8, 2013, **www.pewforum.org/2013/04/08/applying-gods-law-religious-courts-and-mediation-in-the-us/.**

6. Larry Diamond, *Squandered Victory: The American Occupation and the Bungled Effort to Bring Democracy to Iraq* (New York: Henry Holt, 2005).

7. Quakers in the World, "International Mediation and Conciliation," accessed May 14, 2015, **www.quakersintheworld.org/quakers-in-action/210/.**

8. Judith A. Saul, "The Legal and Cultural Roots of Mediation in the United States," *Opinio Juris in Comparatione* 1, no. 8 (2012): 5–6, **www.opiniojurisincomparatione.org/opinio/issue/view/12.**

9. Lao-Tzu, *Tao Te Ching*, verse 17. As quoted by Wayne W. Dyer in *Change Your Thoughts—Change Your Life: Living the Wisdom of the Tao* (Carlsbad, CA: Hay House, 2007), 76.

10. Mediate.com, "Roles of the Mediator," accessed May 14, 2015, **www.mediate.com/divorce/pg31.cfm**.

11. Zena Zumetta, "Styles of Mediation: Facilitative, Evaluative, and Transformative Mediation," Mediate.com, 2000, **www.mediate.com/articles/zumeta.cfm**.

12. Gary Friedman and Jack Himmelstein, "Resolving Conflict Together: The Understanding-Based Model of Mediation," *Journal of Dispute Resolution* 2006, no. 2, article 8 (2006), 523–553, **scholarship.law.missouri.edu/jdr/vol2006/iss2**/8/.

13. Judith A. Saul, "The Legal and Cultural Roots of Mediation in the United States," *Opinio Juris in Comparatione* 1, no. 8 (2012), 8, **papers.ssrn.com/sol3/papers.cfm?abstract_id=2125440**/.

14. FindLaw, "Common Mediation Questions: How Long Does Mediation Typically Take?" accessed May 14, 2015, **adr.findlaw.com/mediation/common-mediation-questions.html**; Center for Resolution of Disputes, "FAQs," 2005, accessed May 14, 2015, **www.cfrdmediation.com/faq.aspx**.

15. Nolo.com, "Divorce Mediation FAQ: How Much Does Mediation Cost?" 2015, accessed May 14, 2015, **www.nolo.com/legal-encyclopedia/divorce-mediation-faq-29035-6.html**; FreeAdvice, "How Much Does Mediation Cost?" 2005, accessed May 14, 2015, **law.freeadvice.com/litigation/mediation/mediation_cost.htm**.

Chapter 2
WHY SHOULD I CHOOSE MEDIATION?

Litigation, n. A machine which you go into as a pig and come out of as a sausage.

—Ambrose Bierce[1]

It's 8:00 p.m. and the new neighbors aren't home. The miniature schnauzer in their apartment has been barking for hours. Your baby had been asleep before the eternal cacophony began, but now baby is screaming and wide awake. Frustrating? Yes! It goes on for hours more. Then finally, peace and quiet returns with the neighbors' arrival home at 11:00.

But the next night, the same thing happens. And then again the next night. And then again. Your neighbors are party animals who hit the clubs right after dinner, but they leave their own animal behind and it goes nuts the minute they're out the door. Six months pass, and the deafening sounds of an unhappy dog still emanate from the neighbors' apartment on a nightly basis.

Finally, one Monday night at 10:30, your baby is screaming in time to the dog's howls. As soon as the neighbors arrive home to pacify their displeased pooch, you get the baby to bed—and you decide you've had enough. Exasperated and angry, you draft a letter to your attorney and the property manager. The barking must stop or you will sue!

The Importance of Addressing the Conflict

In the above example, we put you in the shoes of a parent who spent six months suffering in silence while her neighbors did nothing about their barking dog. Why did she do that? For the same reason most people would: they will do everything possible to avoid addressing a conflict. This mindset is not unique to people in disputes involving animals. When any sort of conflict arises, people usually avoid dealing with it because they know that having a conversation about a conflict is fraught with emotion. If you don't have good conflict resolution skills, talking about the conflict can just inflame emotions and make the situation worse.

This causes people to either hope or assume that the other people they are in conflict with are mind readers. At some point, we've all heard a spouse or partner tell us something like, "If you loved me, you'd know." That person is really telling us, "I want to avoid addressing this conflict, so I expect you to figure it out on your own, and I will get angrier at you if you don't."

Sadly, this dynamic plays out not just in close personal relationships but in all kinds of human interactions. Conflicts are emotional by nature, and when a group of people gets into conflict with another group, they often decide the other group "just doesn't get it"—meaning the other people have failed to be mind readers—and the situation explodes, polarizing the groups. The two groups start acting from a place of anger and defensiveness, they stop communicating, and then the old adage "Let's ignore it—maybe it will go away," kicks in. That only makes the conflict fester more, and then it becomes "my way or the highway" until finally, somebody sues.

The other issue illustrated by the example above is that people in conflict would rather state their position through an intermediary than deal with each other directly. When she hit the end of her rope, the aggrieved parent sent letters to her lawyer and the property manager, wanting them to deal with the situation. She might also have called the city department of animal control and asked them to deal with it. At the same time, however, if she and the dog owners were friends, she might have rung their doorbell, asked them out for a cup of coffee, and not once mentioned the barking dog—not to them.

People just don't want to talk about conflict, especially when the conflict is over a pet. They may decide, based on observation and experience, that pet owners won't listen to anyone who criticizes the behavior of their beloved companion—and if they do listen, their response will be emotional and abusive. The person raising the

> *People just don't want to talk about conflict, especially when the conflict is over a pet.*

criticism about the pet—whether it's a neighbor, a veterinarian, or a dog walker—feels that he or she is simply asking for a favor or expressing concern about the animal's well-being, but the pet owners feel that the criticism is an attack.

Pet lovers often think that non-pet-loving people are social outcasts; after all, they don't like pets. The pet lovers might think, *Isn't there something inherently wrong with people who don't like pets? They're just not normal.* At the same time, non–pet people might feel the same way about pet people, thinking, *These pet people are crazy; after all, it's just an animal.* Also, pet lovers can feel skeptical about people who are involved with their pets professionally because, after all, *Those people are getting paid. They're doing this for money, so they probably have ulterior motives, and they can't possibly understand the way I feel about my pet.*

There is also often fear mixed in with the criticism, and this fear affects all sides. It's the fear of retaliation and the fear of loss. People fear that if they criticize a pet or the pet's owners, those people will retaliate and just make the situation worse. At the same time, pet owners fear that the person complaining about them or their pet will try to have their pet taken away from them or simply pass judgment on them as terrible people. This fear causes people on both sides to work even harder to avoid addressing the conflict, and they often find creative ways of doing so. Six such ways are detailed below.

How People Avoid Addressing the Conflict

Suffering in Silence

This is the method used by the frustrated neighbor in the example at the beginning of this chapter. In fact, people who have an issue with a friend's or neighbor's animal often go this route. The aggrieved parties prefer to avoid all confrontation because they don't want to negatively affect their relationship with a friend or neighbor, so they entirely avoid bringing up the issue with the animal. This tends to backfire on the sufferer. Aggrieved parties who don't speak up continue to suffer. Ignoring the problem just makes it worse. Plus, it can't help but eventually have a negative effect on the friendship with the animal owner.

So even though some religions hold that suffering is good for the soul, I advise against it. Why suffer when a simple conversation may alleviate the problem and save your relationship with your neighbors? That's a much better way of loving your neighbor and doing unto them as you'd have them do unto you.

ESP Communication

This occurs when the people involved in the conflict decide to stop speaking to each other (assuming they have ever spoken at all), opting instead for the mind-reading—or ESP—method of communication. Party A decides to simply wait until Party B guesses or infers, based on Party A's actions and comments, what Party B supposedly should have known all along.

In the long run, this only succeeds in allowing the conflict to fester. It is passive-aggressive behavior that only increases the bad feelings on one or both sides. Party A is not using words to address the problem, while Party B may not even know there is a problem at all. In the end, ESP confrontation is counterproductive because it only further infuriates the party engaging in it.

Venting to Friends and Family

Talking to the person you're angry at is too difficult. After all, what if they get angry back at you? What if they yell at you? What if they say mean things about your pets or your lifestyle or your kids? Or maybe they won't say anything but just give you a hostile glare and a cold shoulder, which can be even worse than being yelled at.

Instead, you talk to your best friend or your sister or your significant other about the problem. They won't yell at you. They won't give you the freeze-out. In fact, they'll undoubtedly be sympathetic because, after all, that's what friends are for.

Why isn't this productive? For one thing, you're putting your confidante in a tough spot. They may believe there's more than one side to the story—since there usually is—but they feel duty bound to support you, no matter how uncomfortable it is for them. For another thing, their words of agreement just validate the point of view you already hold, which is not helping you understand the other dimensions of the situation and work toward a resolution. In fact, when they say, "That's right. You're absolutely right. How dare they say that about your [dog, cat, professional judgment, attitude toward animals …]?! If I were you, I would want to kick that person's ass," you get even more fired up with righteous anger. This takes you even further away from being able to have a calm, open discussion with the person you actually have the conflict with.

Exploding Confrontation

A volatile situation has been building for a while, and then something triggers an explosion. Either the dog started barking in the middle of the night, the parrot used some awful language, the horse ran through your yard again, the cat used your porch couch as a litterbox, or the client didn't pay their bill. If you're the pet owner, maybe the groomer didn't follow your instructions, the veterinarian didn't listen to your pet's history, or your ex fed the cats the wrong food and now they're throwing up. You may have practiced ESP communication up until now, but that just poured gasoline on the kindling. Now the animal or person did something that touched off a spark, and BOOM, you're mad as hell and you're not going to take it anymore!

Once you've exploded, the other person cannot talk to you—at least not reasonably. They may call you unreasonable, crazy, and a pet hater. They may give you testimonials about the love and affection

> *Are you able to look objectively at the issue, or are you blinded by your own anger?*

of everyone else in the area for their pet. They say, "Everyone else likes my dog—why can't you?" thinking that's an ironclad defense against anything you could say. They have no interest in listening to your criticisms, not of their pet or of them as pet owners. They feel attacked, and they think you're just a crazy dog hater or a money-grubbing parasite who can't get along with anyone anyway, so why should they waste their time listening to you?

And yet, you feel so much better now. You've finally gotten to tell those miserable SOBs exactly what you think about them and their %#&@$^! dog, and you've told them exactly what they should do to fix the situation. What a relief! You've gotten it all off your chest, and you feel vindicated because what happened was obviously beyond the pale. Now you've said your piece, and heated though it was, it was the truth and the truth will set you free.

Or will it? After all, whose truth is it? Is it the truth according to you or to everyone involved? Are you able to look objectively at the issue, or are you blinded by your own anger? Have you addressed the conflict, or have you just vented your pent-up rage in a way that has made the conflict worse? Almost certainly you have done the latter. In the end, you're still avoiding addressing the conflict because you're not listening to the other party's perspective. You're just venting at them to justify your own point of view.

Red Rover Confrontation

This occurs when two sides are polarized against each other over an animal-related issue. Words have been exchanged and sides taken. As with the all-encompassing "Everyone loves my pet," defense above, there will be people on one side who love the offending animal or person and people who are annoyed on the other side. The angry parties begin to gather their troops.

In the middle are usually other friends, neighbors, and pet owners. They haven't chosen sides and don't want to, but they're caught up in the conflict anyway because they can't avoid the sense of collective unease caused by a conflict over an animal. Other pet owners often feel their animal is being attacked by association, or they feel like they're being given a choice of supporting an angry neighbor or friend or supporting the accused, whether that is a cute and friendly dog or a trusted veterinarian. They fear that no matter what they do, they will get painted with whatever broad brush gets applied to somebody else. In the end, this polarization will incur untold hardship for everyone, and the conflict will remain totally unaddressed, often with very sad results.

Here is a tragic true story of a Red Rover confrontation. A soap opera actor lived in an apartment building in New York City. His building decided to ban pit bulls, but his own pit bull was grandfathered in. As time went on, he felt the occupants of the building were making snide remarks to him about his dog. Why did he have her in a pit bull–free building? They looked askance at him and his pet. Then his anxiety spilled over onto the dog. She became anxious due to the stress he was under about the polarization in the building. This anxiety changed her personality for the worse, and the actor decided she was no longer safe around people. He had her put to sleep. He gave her toys and bed away to the neighbors. Then he went back to his apartment and committed suicide. He left a note telling the story of this perceived conflict and how it led him to commit suicide. This individual undoubtedly had other problems, but it was his perception of the polarization of the building against him and his dog that caused him to act in a way that led to his own death.

Open, respectful communication avoids this kind of snowballing situation that can lead to tragedy.

Litigation

This is the knee-jerk reaction that many people have in conflicts involving animals. They hire an attorney and sue the pet owner over the rude bird, the filthy feline, or the vocal canine, or they sue the veterinarian or handler due to a poor outcome. They seek to make a novel legal argument and have the pet owner or professional fined.

In real terms, this option may not be of any help. The court picks and chooses its animal issue cases, and the law varies from place to place. If your neighbors let their pet out at 6:00 a.m. and take it in at 10:00 p.m., and if they only allow it to bark

> *Even if you are getting no sleep because of your neighbors' barking dog, the court will have no ability to provide you with recourse.*

incessantly for 14 minutes at a time, they may be in compliance with your city's ordinances. Even if you are getting no sleep because of your neighbors' barking dog, the court will have no ability to provide you with recourse. And that will be after you've paid $1,000 in legal fees, at a minimum.

Litigation is almost always the first route taken in animal conflicts, but it should be the last. It never provides the solution the parties are seeking. It simply involves a third party—the court—in the disagreement for the purpose of deciding the facts and how the law applies. In the process, the court will not consider the relationship between the disputing parties, and it will probably destroy any hope that the relationship can be repaired. Moreover, litigation will do nothing to address the real conflict. In fact, litigation is the most efficient way to avoid addressing the conflict because it turns the conflict over to the courts, which will decide the case based on laws that have nothing to do with the nature and circumstances—including the emotions—of the conflict itself.

WHY NOT LITIGATION?

Pet owners and pet-serving professionals often lose long-term relationships with other people over conflicts involving animals. The relationships become strained, communication becomes difficult if not impossible, and the parties find they have no way to address their disagreement in a safe and respectful way. That is when they go to litigation, expecting the legal system to help them resolve their conflict.

But this is a false hope. The court decides who wins and who loses in a way that is user unfriendly and relationship destructive. The legal system does not support a conversation between the disgruntled parties. It only permits discussions between disinterested legal representatives and the presiding judge. These players apply the law without addressing the emotions that underpin every action brought on behalf of an animal. Litigants in cases involving animals have little reason to pursue conversation, and the court has no interest in reviewing why the parties are suing one another because that issue is beyond the court's scope. The court's job is simply to uncover the facts and apply the law in a way that supports a solution.

If, on the other hand, the litigants had a venue in which to talk to one another respectfully and address the conflict, exploring and resolving the emotions that underpin their grievances, they would no longer have a reason to hire an attorney to speak for them. That is the alternative that a mediator can offer. Instead of going to litigation, people can resolve their conflicts by employing the services of a mediation professional who will bring the disputing parties together so they can engage in a neutrally supported, confidential discussion. The mediator helps the parties have their say in a respectful way, and mediation allows for a more valuable conversation in which solutions can be explored.

> *In fact, even when a dispute is headed to litigation, I tell people to mediate before, during, and after the court proceedings.*

In fact, even when a dispute is headed to litigation, I tell people to mediate before, during, and after the court proceedings. Mediate before to see whether you can avoid litigation. If not, then litigation is still an option. Trying mediation in no way closes that door. Then mediate during litigation to have a confidential reality check that helps both parties have a supported discussion, unlike a negotiation, that helps them understand the issue from the other party's point of view. Sometimes the litigation is about a broader issue, such as a divorce, of which the dispute over the animal is just one part, as when there is a custody battle over the family pet. In such instances, the conflict over the animal can be referred to mediation even while the divorce as a whole is handled through litigation. Finally, if litigation proceeds and the court makes a judgment, mediation can be very helpful in reestablishing a relationship between the parties in the aftermath of that decision so that it can be carried out as respectfully as possible.

Mediation should be the go-to method of resolving highly emotional conflicts. It can help parties in conflict over an animal escape from legal madness. It enables people to have a relationship-saving conversation at the outset of their disagreement. It empowers each person to speak by providing a feeling of safety during a conversation with a perceived adversary. It helps each party find their true voice so that everyone involved can hear and be heard. Because when addressing a conflict over an animal, it's not what you say … it's how you say it.

WHY MEDIATION?

The primary reason to choose mediation in a conflict over an animal is simple: mediation addresses the conflict itself, "not just the facts, ma'am." If the disputing parties come together in mediation to address the conflict, they will have the best chance of speaking about and understanding each other's underlying emotions, which are driving the conflict. They will also have the best chance of coming to a mutually satisfying agreement.

When they come to me, most of my clients are so upset that they can't think about anything but getting their pound of flesh. Something has occurred that has set them off and made them so very angry. The best approach is for me to sit down with both parties, hear them out, and help them come to a resolution. However, I often don't get to sit with both parties. Instead, I have to give conflict coaching to one party, helping him to become a better listener so he can directly resolve the situation with the other party, without litigation. But given my druthers, I will always suggest parties enter into mediation. That's because each party knows the best way to resolve the conflict and, working together, the parties can resolve it in the best interests of the pet.

What Happens in Mediation?

In mediation, the following things can happen:

- Confidential conversation
- Listening and discovery of unknown facts and perceptions
- Clarification and resolution of the conflict
- Preservation of the relationship

Confidential conversation. The best time to start mediation is as soon as possible after a conflict begins. Think about it: When a conflict arises between you and another party, wouldn't it be best to meet ASAP, when you are not yet constantly angry and when you can still speak civilly to each other? Wouldn't it be best to address the conflict by having a cup of coffee, brainstorming about the events that have

> *People can listen to and understand each other while being supported and reflected by the mediator.*

raised the issue, and coming up with a solution that will preserve your relationship? Addressing the issue while it is still fresh and nerves haven't yet been rubbed raw will enable you and the other person to speak openly, nonthreateningly, and nonjudgmentally about your own needs and the pet's needs as well.

A mediator can help you engage in this conversation—the conversation you want to have but don't know how to have. A mediator can help you and the other party address the conflict so you can move forward from conflict to consensus.

Listening and discovery of unknown facts and perceptions. In many cases, people in conflict have a hard time listening to each other. They're so entrenched in their own ideas and point of view, and so busy thinking about what they are going to say next, that they are not listening to the other side. In these cases, mediation is the logical approach to resolving the conflict. Mediation helps the parties by enabling them to get personally involved in addressing their problem together—not avoiding personal involvement as in litigation. A neutral third party brings mediation and coaching skills to both parties while providing them with the space to have their say in a less heated, more respectful way. Then people can listen to and understand each other while being supported and reflected by the mediator.

The mediator is not there to make a decision. Instead, she is there to help people keep talking until they feel heard, respected, and understood. From there, the parties can address the actions that will enable them to go forward more peacefully.

Clarification and resolution of the conflict. In mediation, the parties focus on what they want and not on what the other party wants. By doing this—simply stating how they feel and why they have come to mediation—people can go a long way toward finding common ground. This may seem counterintuitive, yet if the parties focus on what they themselves want, they will gain a clearer understanding of their own issues and how best to resolve them. Often, people in conflict only state their own position as a counter to the other party's argument.

> *As you brainstorm solutions, bits and pieces of the absurd may make sense or help make other solutions possible.*

If they do this, not thinking about what they want and why, then they lose sight of what their own problem is.

If a mediator can get each party to clearly refocus on his or her own individual problem, without getting defensive about the other party's version of the problem, then both parties can find solutions that they never before realized existed. Having a meaningful conversation guided by a mediator—someone who will truly help parties put words to their problems and give form to their conflict—makes a huge difference in whether or not people feel heard.

From clarifying conversations come real solutions. Weird and outlandish solutions may emerge as well, but don't treat them that way. Embrace the absurd—this is how innovative ideas are born. Dismiss nothing. As you brainstorm solutions, bits and pieces of the absurd may make sense or help make other solutions possible. Creative thinking is all about how ideas are perceived, so the mediator encourages everyone to brainstorm freely, without passing judgment on any of the proposed solutions until they're all out on the table. This approach creates an exchange of ideas that neither party had considered before.

But remember, don't rush to solutions. Mediation is not a game of "Beat the Clock." Yes, every hour of mediation costs money, but it's far less money than litigation would involve. The disputing parties in mediation split the mediator's fee, and in exchange for that, they are given equal time to speak, listen, and be heard. It's therefore worth their time and money to commit fully to the mediation process until they have reached a mutually satisfying resolution.

Preservation of the relationship. I give lectures and workshops all over the country, teaching people how to use the right kind of language to have the conversation they've been avoiding. The idea is to help people resolve their conflicts in a way that also resolves the problems in their relationships. In many cases, parties who enter into conflict have a desire to repair and retain the relationship they had before the conflict arose. This is impossible to achieve in litigation—in fact, the litigation process destroys relationships by imposing a legal judgment that doesn't resolve the interpersonal conflict or take into account the emotions that underlie the conflict. Someone will win the case, but both parties will probably lose their relationship, and that does nobody any good—particularly the animal at the center of the dispute. It is therefore better to engage in mediation, a process that puts the relationship between the people and their animals front and center and that takes into account all the emotional needs of the participants. This often results in the preservation of the relationship, as fully described in the next section.

THE GOALS OF MEDIATION: AKA^2—ADDRESS, KEEP, ACKNOWLEDGE & APPRECIATE

Litigation over an animal is often a no-win situation for anyone—especially the animal. In mediation, on the other hand, people in conflict can be heard, understood, and respected, and they can come to the best solution for themselves and for the animal—who is always the most important party involved. I can't overemphasize this last point. In

In effect, mediation elevates a pet from property status to child status.

litigation, the law treats your pet as a thing with no rights, but in mediation, your pet is the most important party, whose interests must be protected—just as the law would protect a child. In effect, mediation elevates a pet from property status to child status if this is what the people involved want. This is exactly what most people do want in a conflict over their beloved pet.

With those priorities established, the goals of mediation are threefold. I like mnemonics, and the one I use to help people remember the goals of mediation is AKA^2—Address, Keep, Acknowledge & Appreciate.

ADDRESS the Conflict

A client walked into my office complaining about neighbors whose dogs had been barking for years. The client had ignored and ignored the barking (suffering in silence), but of course she hadn't really been ignoring it. The issue had actually been festering all that time. I conflict-coached her on how to talk to the neighbors and give them information in a way that was less threatening and less confrontational. It worked like a charm. The neighbors stopped putting the dogs out in front of the house to bark at six o'clock in the morning; instead, they started putting the dogs out back where they didn't bark, or at least no one could hear them.

But then I asked my client if she had written a thank-you note to her neighbors, and the client said no. She said the neighbors had done what they were supposed to do, so why thank them for it? I reminded her that writing a thank-you note was something I had recommended she do, but she insisted it wasn't necessary. Within weeks, the dogs were back out front and barking. Why? Because the neighbors did not feel appreciated for the steps they had taken to resolve the conflict.

This is a classic case of people trying to resolve a conflict without fully addressing the conflict. The emotional issues were still lying there unaddressed, even after the two parties had reached a tenuous solution—and because of that, those emotional issues came back to bite both parties in the form of a renewed conflict.

This is why mediation is so important. Conflict coaching is good, but a conflict-coached client is less likely to fully address the conflict than is a client who sits down in mediation with the other party. Failure to fully address the conflict means it won't be entirely resolved. It may reappear after you think you've resolved it, and it may even get worse.

> *The conflict may reappear after you think you've resolved it, and it may even get worse.*

KEEP the Relationships with Your Pet and the Other Party

> *It's been ten years. Ten years of arguments and unhappiness. It had to come to an end. Everything will be divided right down the middle … except, who gets the dog? Old Rover is the only joyful thing left from the marriage—the playful, snuggly member of the family adored by both owners.*
>
> *The battle over the dog ensues. Lawyers argue: "He walked the dog." "She bathed the dog." "He bought the dog food." "She fed the dog." He said, she said. The battle drags on, and the only people who are happy are the well-paid lawyers.*
>
> *There will be no fairy-tale ending—one person will win and one will lose, but the biggest loser will be the dog. He will lose one caregiver, one human he loves, one of the people he treasures in his life. He didn't take sides, but will there be joint custody? Probably not! Anger and a lack of communication will kill any chance that the dog will have a relationship with both the people he loves—the only situation in which all parties can win.*

When you're in a dispute involving your pet, keeping your relationship with that pet is paramount to you, as it would be to most pet owners. Pets provide us with love, companionship, and safety, and over 85 percent of pet owners classify their pets as companions or members of the family.[2] That means less than 15 percent of current pet owners may think of their pets as property, which is how they are currently seen in the eyes of the law. However, when pets are involved in a conflict between people, maintaining a relationship during and after that conflict is difficult. Whether it is a divorce, an issue with a neighbor, a disagreement with a veterinarian, or another instance in which people are in conflict over an animal, keeping good relationships takes desire and effort.

However, if there is no perceived benefit to getting along with the other party in the future, having a peaceful conversation with them seems pointless. This lack of foresight results in people not making the effort to retain their relationship. Instead, they lock horns and battle to the end because they just don't understand what the fallout will be from their foray into the Pet Wars. If they took the time to think about it, they might both realize that it would make their lives happier or easier if they maintained their relationship, at least enough to take care of their beloved dog. In the example of a divorce, if the man were running late getting home, he would have the option of calling his ex-wife and asking her to go to his place and let out and feed the dog. In that way and many others, life for all—especially the dog—could be a whole lot nicer.

And here's the good news: if you address the conflict through mediation, you will have the best shot at keeping your relationship with all the other parties involved, at least to the extent possible. This is sometimes tougher during a divorce than in any other conflict, but if your pet can keep its relationship with both you and your ex, that is of the greatest importance. Alternatively, if you have a conflict in a dog

> *Do you want to respond negatively, or do you want to create a new reality, one that works for you and the other person?*

park, how do you keep going back there? Or if you have a conflict with a groomer or vet, how do you keep benefitting from this professional's service? What if you are that groomer or vet: How do you keep a long-standing client and avoid the destruction of many other relationships (and potential relationships) when that client smears you all over social media?

By addressing the conflict through mediation, you can keep your relationships alive because you will have given everyone the ability to have a conversation. Then the dog can keep going to the park that is closest or is best for her, or the cat can keep going to the vet who really knows his medical history. But keeping the relationship is never the desire of parties in the midst of litigation, and that's why litigation can be a losing proposition for everyone involved.

So make *Keep the Relationship* your motto. If you truly love your pet, maintaining civility in conversations about the pet's care, both now and in the future, will make things go more smoothly. If you're dealing with someone else who loves their pet, the same thing applies: a civil tone will help preserve the relationship.

If you touch on a sensitive issue about which you cannot speak in a reasonable way, take a deep breath and wait until you've calmed down. Try not to respond; let the other party say all they have to say. Wait and listen. Once they are finished, take your time reflecting back what you heard them say. Make sure you use their words, responding in a reflective way and not with how you feel about what they said. This will make them feel heard and understood, and it will also let you take the time to consider

> *No one can fight with themselves—they need a partner.*

whether you want to remain in conflict with them. Do you want to respond negatively, or do you want to create a new reality, one that works for you and, in return, works for them? The choice you make will either fan or douse the flames of conflict.

No one can fight with themselves—they need a partner—so choose whether or not you want to be in partnership with conflict. A mediator can help you and the other person make the choice not to fight and instead keep the relationship.

ACKNOWLEDGE & APPRECIATE the Other Person's Point of View So You Can Avoid Litigation

Heartbreak! The dog has bone cancer. What can we do?

"Don't despair," says your vet. "I know a specialist who can help. Chemo and radiation will give Buster a good chance at a remission, so let's start the regimen now."

And off you go to the canine oncologist. You'll do anything for your best friend of ten years. But soon, the dog seems weaker and less sturdy. Then, after $10,000 for treatment, the oncologist tells you the chemo didn't work and the leg needs amputation.

Back at your vet's office, he tells you lots of dogs walk on three legs. You've got to make a decision. You've already spent so much money—what can you do now? You don't think sweet old Buster will enjoy life on three legs, so you say no and take him home. Then in just a couple of weeks, he's so weak that you have to put him to sleep. The final insult: after you've paid your vet thousands of dollars for worthless treatments, he charges you for the euthanasia.

That's it! He had to know there was no hope. Why did he let you hope? Why did he take every cent you had? He soaked you. You should sue!

But the vet doesn't understand. He says, "I was just trying to save the dog's life, and now you want to sue me? What's wrong with you?"

In most conflicts involving animals, people fail to appreciate how the other party perceives the unfolding situation. This can be seen in the vet-client misunderstanding above. Each party to this disagreement has failed to appreciate how the other party feels. The family vet recommended what he felt was the best course of action given the pet's prognosis, and that did not mean that if his clients needed additional services at his clinic, he would not charge them for those services. Therefore, the vet sees nothing unusual about charging his clients for euthanasia. The problem in this scenario is that he is not appreciating the clients' emotional fragility after the loss of their pet. For their part, the clients feel they have been giv-en poor information. The vet did not follow up with them on how the dog was progressing, and now he has sent them a bill for the dog's euthanasia, compounding their an-ger over the money they spent for what seems like nothing.

> *The mere fact that you appreciate a differing point of view, no matter how unacceptable you might find it, can cause a shift in the other party's position.*

At the outset of a disagreement, appreciating another party's point of view can be difficult. Walking up to your neighbors and complaining about their dog isn't easy. You believe you have ap-proached the matter in a calm and respectful way, but then they tell you that you have some nerve telling them how to care for their pets. The conversation often deteriorates into accusations that have little to do with the problem animal. One party is accused of hating animals, while the other is called an incompetent pet owner. This type of combative exchange does not invite participation in a solu-tion-oriented conversation about an animal's behavior. So if you truly want to settle the argument in the best interests of all involved, start by acknowledging and appreciating the other party's point of view and actions.

If you appreciate why people think what they think and do what they do, it enables you to understand them—and with that un-derstanding comes the opportunity for dialogue. Dialogue provides an opportunity for change. Through dialogue, your position may shift, or it may remain unchanged. Either way, the mere fact that you appreciate a differing point of view, no matter how unacceptable you might find it, can cause a shift in the other party's position. They may become less defensive, and that can cause your conversations to become more constructive.

Be aware that appreciating the other side's point of view does *not* mean you agree with it. It simply creates a starting point from which to have a constructive conversation. For example, you can start by appreciating that your neighbors like to have quiet time in the morning by drinking coffee out on their deck before they go to work. Therefore, you should acknowledge that since your dog barks at them when they are on their deck, they feel you should bring your dog inside in the mornings. Making that acknowledgment doesn't mean you agree with them—it just means you can see their point of view. If you do this, then you can ask them to acknowledge and appreciate the fact that you need the dog to be out in the yard in the morning so he can work off his energy and thus not be destructive inside the house after you leave for work. If they will acknowledge and appreciate that, then you and your neighbors will have acknowledged and appreciated each other's points of view. From there, you can begin to work out a reasonable solution that takes both your points of view into account.

All of this can be facilitated by a mediator, and the mediator will also make sure that the parties listen—both to each other and themselves. People who listen to themselves while they talk out their feelings will get a better understanding of why the situation is a problem for them, and people who listen to the other party will be able to appreciate and acknowledge their point of view. Doing all this will help the ensuing conversation run its course in a productive way. It is in listening, not talking, that common ground is found.

PUTTING IT ALL TOGETHER

During mediation, some people come up with original and even bizarre solutions to their conflicts. It doesn't matter—we mediators put everyone's proposed solutions up on a board and hear them out, no matter how outlandish they are. We do this because everyone's desires need to be acknowledged and respected. Once we do this, the parties are usually surprised at how many of the solutions from the opposing side are similar or identical to their own. In fact, to appreciate each

> *Via social media, conflicts over animals can take on a life of their own and go viral, so why make your own life miserable?*

and every one of the solutions that the parties have is tantamount to resolution of their conflict. Through this brainstorming, the parties can avoid litigation.

I can't tell you how many of my clients walk into my office and start mediation "knowing" that they're going into litigation because there's no way they're going to find a solution—and walk out with a resolution that meets all of their needs in far less time, for far less money, while keeping their relationship alive. Once again, keeping relationships alive is of paramount importance. You don't want to pull out of your driveway and not be able to wave to your neighbor, and you don't want to go to the dog park and not be part of the group that you've seen there every morning for years. Furthermore, in any emotional conflict like one over animals, the last thing you want to be is the bad guy—especially in this day and age. Via social media, conflicts over animals can take on a life of their own and go viral, so why make your own life miserable? Just use mediation to come to a mutually satisfactory solution, and then you'll keep your human relationships and maybe even improve them.

If you thought there were only two ways to deal with conflicts over animals—ignoring the conflict or litigation—then this section has provided you with a third option: using a mediator to resolve the conflict by letting both you and the party you're in conflict with be heard, respected, and understood.

1. Ambrose Bierce, *The Devil's Dictionary*, ed. David E. Schultz and S. T. Joshi (1906; Athens: University of Georgia Press, 2000), p. 152.

2. S. P. Cohen, "Can Pets Function as Family Members? *Western Journal of Nursing Research* 24 (2002), 621–638, as cited in Froma Walsh, "Human-Animal Bonds II: The Role of Pets in Family Systems and Family Therapy," *Family Process* 48, no. 4 (2009), 481, **www.kenrodogtraining.com/upload/human.pdf**.

Chapter 3
MEDIATION WORKS!

It would seem that common sense and reason ought to find a way to reach agreement in every conflict of honest interests.

—Henry James[1]

In November 2013, a New York court issued an opinion in *Travis v. Murray*, a case involving the division of property from a very short marriage. On its face, there was little to distinguish this case from many others, but in the matter of the decision regarding the family dog, it was truly groundbreaking. For the first time, the judge in a divorce case wrote at length of today's changing attitudes toward pets and how those new attitudes have run up against the harsh realities of litigation (see box).

To me, the outcome of *Travis v. Murray* was heartbreaking. The decision guaranteed that one of the owners would lose Joey forever and that Joey would never enjoy his relationship with her again. Plus, the adversarial final hearing would destroy any chance that the divorcing spouses could salvage a continuing relationship that would allow them to help each other take care of Joey. Lastly, despite acknowledging that society is moving toward the idea that pets are people too, the court set a precedent in New York dismissing the idea that pets should have their best interests taken into account and rejecting the idea that pet custody disputes should be given the same time and resources as child custody disputes. In the end, all the judge did was give the parties to the divorce one extra day to argue over who had a better claim to the pet, with the court to make the final determination if the parties could not agree.

Therefore, despite his best efforts not to do so, the judge ended up treating the dog as little better than property because the law wouldn't allow him do anything else. That's why going to litigation over a pet doesn't work.

TRAVIS V. MURRAY[2]

[In the] first divorce case I heard involving a dog ... the ex-wife ... filed a motion seeking an order giving her "full custody" of the dog. During the same time period, the February 1, 2010, issue of *New York* magazine hit the newsstand. The magazine's cover featured a photograph of a Boston terrier staring up with a face exhibiting equal parts bemusement and bewilderment. Like many of us, the dog was no doubt considering the question that appeared next to the photograph: "A Dog Is Not a Human Being, Right?"

With its finger on the pulse of our collective New York psyche, the issue's lead story, "The Rise of Dog Identity Politics," vividly described a canine-centric city where dogs play an ever more important role in our emotional lives.... It detailed many aspects of what the writer referred to as the "humanification" of our pets.... [Then] with a new canine case before me, another of New York City's major publications ran an opinion piece examining the unique relationship between dogs and people. The piece, "Dogs Are People, Too," which appeared in the Sunday Review section of *The New York Times,* urges that dogs be granted what the author calls "personhood."

The earlier *New York* magazine story and the more recent *Times* opinion piece highlight the distinct trend towards looking at dogs as being far more than property, a trend that has only intensified over the last few years.... [But] neither of the two articles mentions dog custody.... What is even more surprising, considering New Yorkers' dedication to their dogs and their propensity for litigation, is that there are so few reported cases from the courts of this state dealing with pet custody in general and no cases at all making a final award of a pet to either side in the context of a divorce. As a result, courts are left with little direction with respect to questions surrounding dog custody: Can there be such a thing as "custody" of a canine? If so, how is a determination to be made? And if not, how does the court decide what happens when a couple divorces and each of them wants the beloved dog as her own?

[In this case,] both sides invoke two different approaches in determining which one should be awarded [the dog] Joey. The first approach is the traditional property analysis, with plaintiff maintaining that Joey is her property by virtue of having bought him and defendant maintaining that the dog is hers as a result of plaintiff having gifted him to her. The second approach is the custody analysis, with each side calling into play such concepts as nurturing, emotional needs, happiness and, above all, best interests—concepts that are firmly rooted in child custody analyses.

Thus the judge laid out the legal background and cultural environment of the case, plus the legal avenues both parties had chosen. Then the judge went on at length, analyzing each party's approach and how it related to existing case law. However, despite making a heroic effort to find a way of treating the dog as something more than mere property, the judge came to this conclusion:

> After reviewing the progression of the law in both New York and other states, it can be concluded that in a case such as this, where two spouses are battling over a dog they once possessed and raised together, a strict property analysis is neither desirable nor appropriate. Although Joey the miniature dachshund is not a human being and cannot be treated as such, he is decidedly more than a piece of property, marital or otherwise. As a result, whether plaintiff bought Joey from the pet store with her own funds or whether defendant received him from plaintiff as a gift is only one factor to consider when determining what becomes of him.
>
> But if not a strict property analysis, what should be the process by which Joey's fate is decided and what standard should be applied in making that determination? Should the court adopt a custody analysis similar to that used for child custody? And if so, is the well-established standard of "best interests of the child" to be replaced by that of "best interests of the canine"?
>
> The majority of cases from other jurisdictions … have declined to extend child custody precepts to dog disputes. Some have been plainly dismissive (see

e.g. *Desanctis v. Pritchard*, 803 A2d 230, 232 [Pa Super Ct 2002] [shared custody of a dog, Barney, not permissible because he is personal property and as such, said arrangement would be "analogous, in law, to (custody of) a table or a lamp"]) ... [and] with the exception of *Placey*, the Alabama case, even the decisions employing custody or custody-like considerations to dog disputes have uniformly rejected the application of a "best interests" standard....

Even if there were a method to readily ascertain in some meaningful manner how a dog feels, and even if a finding could be made with regard to a dog's best interests, it is highly questionable whether significant resources should be expended and substantial time spent on such endeavors. It is no secret that our courts are overwhelmed with child custody cases, cases in which the happiness and welfare of our most precious commodity, children, are at stake. To allow full-blown dog custody cases, complete with canine forensics and attorneys representing not only the parties but the dog itself, would further burden the courts to the detriment of children. Such a drain of judicial resources is unthinkable.

This does not mean, however, that cases like this one, in which it appears that each spouse views the dog as a family member and sincerely believes that he would be better off in her care, should be given short shrift.... With this in mind, it is appropriate that the parties here be given a full hearing. "Full" does not mean extended; the hearing shall not exceed one day. The standard to be applied will be what is "best for all concerned," the standard utilized in *Raymond*. In accordance with that standard, each side will have the opportunity to prove not only why she will benefit from having Joey in her life but why Joey has a better chance of living, prospering, loving, and being loved in the care of one spouse as opposed to the other.

At this juncture, it should be made clear that, absent an appeal, the one-day hearing to determine who gets Joey will be the final proceeding on this issue. The award of possession will be unqualified. This means that whichever spouse is awarded Joey will have sole possession of him to the complete exclusion of the other. Although regrettably a harsh and seemingly unfeeling outcome, it is the only one that makes sense. As has been stated, our judicial system cannot extend to dog owners the same time and resources that parents are entitled to in child custody proceedings. The extension of an award of possession of a dog to include visitation or joint custody—components of child custody designed to keep both parents firmly involved in the child's life—would only serve as an invitation for endless post-divorce litigation, keeping the parties needlessly tied to one another and to the court.... While children are important enough to merit endless litigation, as unfortunate as that litigation may be, dogs, as wonderful as they are, *simply do not rise to the same level of importance* [emphasis mine].

So there you have it. In one decision, the judge determined that while dogs deserve to be treated as more than just property, the court system simply doesn't have the time, the resources, or even the ability to do it. Instead, the judge sent the divorcing spouses to an adversarial one-day hearing in which each spouse would have to argue why she would be better qualified to be the dog's sole owner. The judge stated that this was the only solution that made sense, despite admitting that it was harsh and unfeeling. While the judge briefly considered the best interests of the dog, he ended up throwing out the very concept of a pet's best interests as unascertainable by the court.

MEDIATION IS *NOT* NEGOTIATION (NO MATTER WHAT YOUR LAWYER SAYS)

I found the court's decision in *Travis v. Murray* heartbreaking for other reasons as well. First, had mediation been used in the case, the ownership and visitation rights could have been decided in a way that would have put the best interests of Joey first and that would have allowed both parties to be a part of Joey's life going forward. Second, no court precedent would have been set denying litigants the right to have their pet treated as more than property, so future litigants might not have suffered the consequences of that precedent. Third—and most importantly to me—I could have done something about it, had I only been given the opportunity. You see, I know one of the attorneys who litigated *Travis v. Murray*, and when I heard about the judge's decision, I called the attorney and asked, "Why didn't you ask to mediate the piece about the dog?" She said, "Oh, I did mediate it." And I asked, "How did you do that if you were the lawyer for one of the parties in the case?" And she said, "Well, I'm a mediator, so I know how to mediate."

And that's the problem: Most attorneys don't understand what mediation is, so they don't see the value of bringing in a mediation professional like me. They think mediation is just negotiation—and as lawyers, they negotiate all the time, so they think they can run mediations as well. However, negotiation and mediation are two very different things. In negotiation, two parties declare what they want from each other and then bargain with each other until each party gets enough from the other to strike a deal, both leaving un-happy. Once the deal is done, the parties walk away from the table and may never speak to each other again. They certainly don't address

Negotiation and mediation are two very different things.

the conflict between them—and why should they? They're just look-ing to get whatever they can from the other party, and their relation-ship (if any) is not even discussed, much less preserved.

But mediation is all about addressing the conflict and preserv-ing the relationship between the disputing parties. Moreover, in a dispute involving an animal, it's also about preserving the relation-ship both parties have with the animal. A lawyer for one of those parties can't do that because by definition, the lawyer isn't neutral. A mediator, on the other hand, has to be neutral; the mediator has to support both sides in the mediation. If either party thinks the medi-ator is on the other party's side, then the mediation will immediately break down. Thus, there's no way a lawyer representing a client in litigation can run a mediation between his client and the other par-ty. The lawyer must bring in a neutral mediation professional.

And then there's something even more basic: negotiation is about going back and forth with the other party until you reach an agreement, but mediation is about shutting up and listening to the other party until you understand his point of view since that's how you address the conflict.

Now I don't know if you've been to Staples lately, but they've got a lot of really colorful duct tape with pictures of animals on it. During my introduction to any mediation, I always put a roll of that duct tape out on the table—not because I'm kinky, but because I want to explain to the parties that we're all there to listen to each other. Then I tell them that if I ever feel the urge to interrupt them and tell them what to do, I'm going to pick up that roll of duct tape and think to myself, *If I say a word, I'm going to have to slap a piece of this duct tape over my mouth!* I tell both parties that I'd like them to do the same. I remind them that they're both going to get equal time, so if they ever feel like interrupting while the other party is talking, they should pick up the duct tape and get ready to slap a piece of that tape over their mouth.

Now just think if you picked up a magazine and saw a cartoon in it of three people sitting at a table—one taking notes, one talking, and one with a piece of duct tape with penguins on it slapped over his mouth—with a caption below it saying, "NEGOTIATION." You'd laugh and probably ask what the cartoonist was smoking, because obviously, that's not what negotiation is. But it's definitely what mediation is: one party mediating, one party speaking, and one party listening and not interrupting—by any means necessary—until the person talking is done talking. Only then does the speaking party—who has said what they have to say—pick up the duct tape so the formerly listening party can start talking.

This dynamic is something lawyers don't understand, and that's why you need to talk to a mediation professional if you're in a dispute over an animal. Only in mediation can you address your conflict in a way that puts the best interests of your animal first (something the judge in the decision above said was impossible for the courts to do). And only in mediation is that conversation confidential, giving you the best chance of preserving your relationship with the other person in the dispute as well as with your pet.

MEDIATION *IS* ABOUT SAVING AND KEEPING RELATIONSHIPS

While litigation can destroy relationships and negotiation fails to fully address conflicts, mediation addresses the problem so the disputing parties can save their relationship, hopefully with each other and definitely with the pet. In fact, saving and keeping relationships is what mediation is all about.

Most people call me saying they never want to speak to their neighbor with the barking dog again, but then I ask what the relationship was like before the dog started barking. They may still say that they never want to speak to their neighbor again, but then I ask, "Wouldn't it be nicer for everyone in the neighborhood if the two of you weren't at each other's throats?" That's a reality check that gets them thinking. They've been friends for twenty years and this dog has been barking for two years, and now the situation has exploded and they're never going to speak to each other again. But they have a lot of history together, so I ask them to think about what has been lost and what could be gained.

> *Especially in smaller communities or close-knit professions, it's so much easier on everyone if the disputing parties can preserve their relationship.*

While I don't force people to retain their relationships, if they insist that they never want to speak to each other again, I always ask them to confirm that the relationship really isn't worth saving. Even if they swear up and down that the relationship isn't worth saving, after they've addressed the conflict in mediation and felt heard, understood, and respected by the other party, they sometimes say, "You know, maybe I will talk to her after all, because she really did listen to me and respect where I was."

Especially in smaller communities or close-knit professions, it's so much easier on everyone if the disputing parties can preserve their relationship. For neighbors with barking dogs or breeders and owners and handlers who go to dog shows together, it's all about retaining the relationships. While people shouldn't retain the relationship if they can't do it with an open heart and a clear conscience, if they can, then they should.

MEDIATION GETS RESULTS

So how does all of this work in real life? Well, I listen to people's stories for a living, so let me take a rare chance to tell you some stories of my own that show mediation works. Mediation saves relationships, and it's immensely valuable to professionals like veterinarians because it can keep them from getting sued and having their license put at risk.

Owners and Veterinarians

Once I worked with a veterinarian who had tried and failed to save a dog, leaving the owner out of his mind with grief. The vet called me, saying that while his insurance company wanted him to not talk to the owner, he knew that he could talk the owner down from suing him if he just had the chance. His reason for this was simple: he didn't want to risk his license. You see, every time a veterinarian is sued, his or her license gets reviewed by the state veterinary board— something that no licensed professional wants.

Luckily, this vet had heard me give a talk in which I'd explained how he should handle his insurance company. I explained that if veterinarians go to their insurance company and say they need to mediate a dispute with a client, the insurance company will say, "There's nothing to mediate because your client hasn't sued you yet." I tell them to tell the insurance company, "I know, but I don't want them to sue me because I don't want my license put into play, and I'd also like to keep this client. So I'd like to mediate now so they never sue me." Unfortunately, the insurance company will say, "Well, we don't do that."

I'm trying to change that paradigm. Some insurance companies tell me, "Well, we'd just like the vet to talk to the pet owners." And I say, "No, you don't, because the beauty of mediation is that it's confidential. Let's say the veterinarian or even the pet owner says something stupid in mediation. It can't be used against him or her if a lawsuit is filed. Plus, if the vet talks to a pet owner on his own and says something stupid, the pet owner can make the stupid thing the vet said go viral on social media."

Now compare that to a mediation I did between a vet and a longtime client in which the two parties worked out their disagreement and the client ended up becoming the vet's biggest fan on Facebook—writing tributes that said, "I had a big disagreement with Dr. X., and Dr. X actually hired the mediator and we split the payment, and it was much cheaper for me than litigating and suing him, and it was much better for him because I stayed a client of his. He actually got to hear me out, and the mediator got us to talk to each other, and I actually got to tell the vet what I thought of him. And like, that's perfect!" That never would have happened if the situation had gone to litigation since the vet and the client never would have talked to each other. In that case, she would have gone on social media and kicked the crap out of him. While litigation would have destroyed the relationship between the veterinarian and the client, mediation saved the relationship and even wildly improved it.

I worked on another case in which a young woman brought her dog to an emergency clinic and on the intake papers, it said not to use a certain type of medication. The dog had an autoimmune disease, and if the vet used that medication, the warning said it would send the dog into orbit. The vet read the medication warning and understood it. However, the dog was in such a crisis that the vet had to use that medication to save the dog's life. Therefore, he used the drug he wasn't supposed to use and thereby saved the dog's life, and everybody was happy that night. About 36 hours later, however, the dog crashed and ended up in the emergency room at a different clinic, one by the owner's home. The vets there—delightful as they were—said, "Oh, the vet at the other clinic used this drug and he never should have."

It's unfortunate that they said that because, quite frankly, they were not there. The vets at the second clinic didn't know why the vet at the first clinic had used that drug. Maybe he was unwise to use it, but why not call him and ask why he'd used it before throwing him under the bus? Plus …

The owner wanted to talk to the vet at the first clinic, and he wanted to talk to her—but the emergency clinic where the vet worked wouldn't allow it. And …

When I called the vet's insurance company, they informed me that they only go to mediation after a lawsuit is commenced. If a lawsuit isn't filed, they said, then they never mediate because there's no need. Now the reasons for that are simple: First, an insurance company doesn't need to defend a vet if a pet owner has not filed a claim. Second, if the pet owner has filed a claim, then the insurance company reviews the incident and may find it without merit. In that case, the company will dismiss it outright without payment. Then if the pet owner sues, the company will ask the court for a

Vets in conflict with their clients have to talk to their clients to save the relationship.

summary judgment and, from the company's point of view, there is still no reason for them to discuss the matter with the client or for the vet to talk to the client. The insurance company has no stake in the emotions involved or the vet-client relationship.

Well, that's BS! It leaves vets in a bind because there's an oversupply of vets and most vets want to keep all of their clients. Vets in conflict with their clients need the ability to talk to their clients in order to save the relationship. In the case of this emergency vet, he really just wanted to talk to the owner about why he did what he did, which saved the dog's life at the time.

The vet's insurance company never did let the vet talk to the client, so I ended up speaking to the two parties separately. I obtained written permission from the vet and the pet owner to speak to the other confidentially, and I relayed what each person told me to the other. I told the client that the vet had told me he thought the dog wouldn't make it through the night without the drug he wasn't supposed to use. That's why he used it, and the dog did make it through the night. Even though the dog crashed 36 hours later, he was stronger at that point than he would have been had he not gotten the banned medication, and that's why the new clinic was able to save the dog after he crashed. In other words, there was a valid reason why the vet had used the drug.

Upon hearing that, the client told me that he'd never wanted to sue the vet. He'd just wanted to find out why the vet had done what he did so if the vet had made a mistake, a similar situation would never happen again. I told all this to the vet, and in the end, the two parties worked out their differences through me, a confidential, neutral intermediary. And nobody got sued or had his license reviewed.

The Owner and the Breeder

Puppies sometimes get sick, and breeders can get really angry with puppy owners when that happens. Breeders often feel that owners do not take care of their dogs properly, so they blame the owners for the puppies' illness. However, the fact is that owners usually do the best they can for their puppies. Furthermore, breeders don't always keep in contact with owners to advise them on how to care for their puppies.

In one situation in which I was the mediator, the breeder didn't keep in contact with the owner, and the owner didn't make an effort to call the breeder either. The dog got sick because the owner didn't think that feeding the puppy the right food was important. When the breeder finally heard about the situation, he came down on the owner like a ton of bricks, providing a clue to why the owner had never called the breeder: the breeder was a know-it-all with lousy customer service skills. There was plenty of blame to go around.

Now when a dog owner gets a new puppy, the breeder needs be authoritative in telling the owner how to care for the dog, but he or she should not be condescending. The breeder should think about bringing the new owner along on the journey of raising the puppy, rather than just dictating to the new owner how to care for the puppy. Admittedly, there's a fine line between educating the owner and dictating, and one way or another, the breeder has to make the owner understand that he or she really does need to do certain things to take proper care of the puppy.

This breeder didn't educate the owner and the owner stopped calling, and the puppy got sick. The dog didn't fully recover from its illness and then had difficulty walking, so the owner wanted his money back from the breeder for selling a faulty dog. However, the breeder said, "Well, you didn't feed it the food I told you to, and you didn't follow the vaccination protocol I told you to, so forget it." A lawsuit was looming.

> *In the end, the owner and the breeder split the costs of the dog's care, and the dog ended up recovering fully.*

I was called in because neither party really wanted to litigate but neither party wanted to settle either—they both wanted their pound of flesh. We did mediation, and in the end, the owner and the breeder split the costs of the dog's care, and the dog ended up recovering fully. We got to this outcome because during mediation, it emerged that it is really important for breeders to take the time to speak to owners so that owners don't feel inadequate to raising their dogs. That's the biggest problem owners have with breeders: they don't want to call the breeders because they don't want to hear what they've done wrong. Breeders don't necessarily keep in touch either, figuring it's the owner's responsibility to call if there's a problem, and then when something goes wrong with the dogs, the breeders become argumentative. While a breeder will tell the owner what's best for the dog, the breeder may not communicate that information in a way that's respectful of the owner, who is frightened and feels inadequate and doesn't want to be yelled at. So while breeders should be educating owners about how to get great results with their dogs, the breeders can come across as talking down to the owners or chastising them, and that of course causes the owners to withdraw from communication because they don't want to be talked to that way.

But this case had a happy ending. The dog got better because the breeder called me and said, "You've got to get involved here because the dog's not going to get better." So I did. Key here was my explaining carefully to the owner that I was not the breeder's friend. I made it clear that I was a mediator and that I didn't have any stake in the situation other than wanting to help the dog—which I confirmed was the most important thing to both the owner and the breeder. During mediation, we worked out that if the owner had called the breeder sooner, the dog would have been treated sooner and the disease symptoms would have been relieved sooner. At the same time, we worked out that the breeder had not kept in touch with the owner and had not given the owner the confidence needed to deal with the breeder without feeling inadequate and intimidated. That's how we worked out the cost-sharing arrangement that resulted in a common-ground solution for both parties: the dog should get proper treatment so it can recover and be healthy.

And nobody got sued or lost their dog.

The Owner and the Horse Barn

A horse barn had a client who wasn't paying his bills, and all the other clients ganged up on him. The delinquent client said he wasn't leaving and that the other clients would have to evict him if they wanted him out. Then one of the clients called me, saying she wanted me to represent her and the rest of them as they sought to get the delinquent client out. I told her I don't do litigation but that I could help her have a conversation with the delinquent client, so we went to mediation.

After we sat down and the delinquent client started talking, it turned out that he had the money to pay his bills but felt totally alienated from the other horse owners. His bad feelings went back to a time soon after he joined the horse barn. He had gone riding with all of them, and they had reacted poorly to him. After he was done talking, the other horse owners had their chance to talk, and it turned out they all thought he was a pain because he was very opinionated and didn't observe barn etiquette. They thought his horse was a pain, too, because it had a personality conflict with another horse. That's why after one ride with him, they had never invited him to go riding with them again. In turn, he felt wronged by their ostracizing him, and that's why he wasn't paying his bill.

So in the beginning, we had gone to mediation because the other horse owners thought that if they agreed to mediate, they'd be able to get the delinquent horse owner out. In mediation, however, the rest of the horse owners were able to tell him what they'd wanted to tell him all along: "You know, we don't mind if you come riding with us, but we want you to shut up. You talk too much, and you don't clean up after yourself in the barn, and you seem to expect all of us to clean up after you when you leave the barn a mess." They were able to say that in a safe environment, and he was able to hear them and reply, "I had no idea I left all my stuff out. I had no idea I was so loud that I scared people's horses. I had no idea that my horse didn't get along with that horse and that these are all the reasons nobody invited me to go with them after that first ride."

The delinquent horse owner had really wanted to engage in a conversation with the other horse owners, but they hadn't been engaging with him—they had just wanted him out. Not only that, but he actually liked the other people in the barn, even though he thought they were weird and rude. And guess what: they admitted they had been weird and rude! Horse barns are like dog parks in that they're some of the worst places for producing conflicts between animal owners. If your horse bites or kicks or if your horse doesn't like other horses, then everybody else will want you out, and they probably won't want to talk to you about why they want you out. That's exactly why you have to talk to each other. In fact, after the people in the horse barn finally did talk in mediation, not only did the delinquent horse owner not leave, but he became a more appropriate—and more welcome—member of the barn. He cleaned up after himself, made his horse behave better, and generally tried not to act like a pain around the others. If he did, the other owners gave him some good-natured guidance, and everyone behaved more appropriately. This is another case of a relationship not just being saved but actually being strengthened through mediation.

I still laugh about this when I remember one of the horse owners telling me, "Whatever we do, we just want to get him out." And I said, "Well, I'm just here to listen to your stories." I always say that, because I really do love to hear people's stories. Then they talk and talk, and while they're doing that, the other people in the room are hearing how they feel. In this case, the delinquent horse owner really felt that everybody else was mean to him. They responded, "No, we're not mean." And I said, "Wait a minute, I'm not saying you are mean, but that's how he feels, so let's hear him out." And that's why mediation works: everybody gets to be heard and have their feelings acknowledged and respected, and everyone ends up understanding how everyone else feels. When that happens, it gives the parties the ability to start addressing the conflict and start repairing their relationship.

1. Henry James, "The Moral Equivalent of War," in *"The Moral Equivalent of War" and Other Essays, and "Selections from Some Problems of Philosophy"* (1906; New York: Harper & Row, 1971), p. 6.

2. *Travis v. Murray*, 2013 NY Slip Op 23405 [42 Misc 3d 447], November 29, 2013, Cooper, J., Supreme Court, New York, County, as corrected through Wednesday, February 12, 2014, **www.courts.state.ny.us/reporter/3dseries/2013/2013_23405.htm**.

Self-Assessment 1

A MEDITATION ON MEDIATION

If someone said the word *mediation* to you, what thoughts or images would come to mind?

_____

_____

_____

_____

Have your ideas about mediation changed after reading Section One of this book? If so, how?

_____

_____

_____

_____

Think about a recent conflict situation. How do you tend to deal with conflict now?

_____

_____

_____

_____

(continued)

How do your current methods of dealing with conflict usually work out for you?

_____

_____

_____

_____

How do you think you might use mediation to resolve conflict?

_____

_____

_____

_____

What questions do you still have about mediation?

_____

_____

_____

_____

Section Two
HOW MEDIATION WORKS

Near the beginning of any mediation, I usually tell the story about how the firefighters would come talk to us in grade school. This was in the 1960s, just when polyester first hit the market. Clothes made with the new fabric were wonderful … except that when you walked by an open flame, your clothes caught on fire. Prudently, the school brought in firefighters to teach us what to do when our clothes went up in flames:

STOP, DROP, and ROLL!

That's what you had to do to put the fire out: stop running, drop to the floor, and roll around to put the flames out—because if you just kept running willy-nilly through the house with your clothes on fire, you'd burn to a crisp.

I tell my clients that when they're in conflict, it's like being on fire. In fact, it's like the other party in the conflict is a fire-breathing dragon setting them on fire. That's why I say, "When someone says something to you that's really horrible, just remember my calming voice telling you, 'STOP, DROP, and ROLL.'" I've had so many clients call me back, text me, or email me saying, "OMG, I nipped a conflict in the bud because just like you said, I STOPPED, DROPPED, and ROLLED."

You're probably sitting there thinking, *What does this have to do with conflicts over animals?* Well, as you know, if you respond in kind to an attack, conflict accelerates. In fact, the accelerant for conflict is the act of engaging others in the same hostile manner in which they are engaging you. However, conflict cannot accelerate if there is no accelerant, so what I teach in my workshops is how to have conversations that don't accelerate conflict. You do that by taking the time to STOP, DROP, and ROLL.

Now don't take this literally—I don't tell my clients to start break dancing when somebody starts to criticize them. That might turn them into instant YouTube celebrities, but it wouldn't help them address their conflict. Instead, I use the metaphor of STOP, DROP, and ROLL to help them understand that they must immediately do what's necessary to put out the flames of conflict before the fire gets out of control. Only then can they address the conflict in a way that preserves their relationship with the other people involved.

I've had STOP, DROP, and ROLL work for every kind of conflict involving animals. I've had parrots that were rude, making people want to sue each other over what the parrots said. I've had horses run through yards, creating conflicts between neighbors. I've had conflicts among dog breeders/owners/handlers who avoided addressing the problems for years, letting them fester and escalate due to lack of communication. I've had neighbors with barking dogs, which along with divorce is the biggest reason people call me. I've had trainers and pet suppliers come to me for conflict coaching because they needed help with their customer interactions.

I've even had it work for me in my own practice. As a legal professional, I know that when someone calls into question my ability to practice law, my first response is to defend myself, saying, "Are you kidding? I'm the attorney here. I know the law. I know how this is going to proceed. I know how people and judges and courts work." It gets my dander up, and if I follow my gut instincts, I will jump into the fray and start telling you just how smart I am. That's why STOP, DROP, and ROLL is so important to nipping the conflict in the bud, and that's why having a mediation strategy is important to resolve the conflict and retain your relationship with the other party.

If you're a veterinarian and client comes into the clinic irate about how you treated his pet, how do you deal with him? Or if you're a pet owner and the professional you're dealing with is not being professional, how do you deal with her? Or even if you're a non–pet owner and you're being constantly annoyed by other people's pets, how do you keep those people from thinking you're a pet hater (something pet owners often think of non–pet owners)? To that end, I've incorporated the ideas we've discussed so far in this book into six tactics that I use in mediation. I present them here so you can understand how mediation works. You'll recognize tactics 4 through 6 from the discussion of the goals of mediation in Chapter 2.

DEBRA'S 6 TACTICS FOR CONFLICT MEDIATION

1. STOP talking and listen.
2. DROP the need to be right.
3. Let what the other party says ROLL off your back.
4. ADDRESS the conflict.
5. KEEP the relationship.
6. ACKNOWLEDGE and APPRECIATE the other party.

Chapter 4
TACTIC 1: STOP

It was impossible to get a conversation going; everybody was talking too much.

—Yogi Berra[1]

WHAT DOES STOP MEAN?

In the parlance of resolving conflicts over animals, STOP means *just stop talking and listen*. The first reason to STOP is simple: it's very hard to fight with someone who isn't fighting back. Replying in kind to attacks just encourages more attacks, but sitting peacefully and listening has the opposite effect. If you just listen to all of the other party's complaints and demands, then the other party will run out of steam after they've gotten

> *It's important to keep in mind that to stop and listen does not mean giving up or giving in.*

all the anger out of their system. After venting all that anger, they will be more likely to STOP and listen to you in return. Also, it's important to keep in mind that to STOP and listen does *not* mean giving up or giving in—it simply means taking the time to hear what the other party has to say, without retaliating.

The second reason to STOP is that when you listen, you can begin to hear what the real issue is. When you're busy thinking about what you're going to say in answer to what they're saying, you can never hear what the real issue is. Plus, your answers to what the other person says will likely be driven by your own preconceived biases about the situation and the person you're in conflict with. Ultimately, you'll jump to conclusions that have nothing to do with the reality of the situation, and that's a recipe for disaster because it's just another way to avoid addressing the conflict.

In contrast, to STOP talking and just listen creates a starting point from which to address the conflict. It lets you take the time to truly understand how the other party's point of view differs from yours and what the root of the conflict really is. Plus, it's often in the middle of a tirade that the other party will say something that clues you in to their true feelings. For example, if you are a vet and a pet has been harmed in your clinic, you may assume that the pet owner just wants to prove that you are responsible for that harm. However, if you STOP and listen, you may hear the pet owner say or imply that she just wants to understand what happened and make sure the same thing doesn't happen to another pet. If that's the deep-seated feeling she has and the resolution she most dearly wants, then if you STOP and listen to her, you will hear the pain she is going through, the steps she wants you to take to ensure the situation never happens again, and her desire to be included in the creation of that solution.

The third reason to STOP is that by listening, you will enable the other party to be heard and *feel* that you have heard them. It is very important that they feel you have completely heard them out and that you appreciate and acknowledge their point of view. Only then will they be open to hearing you out so they can understand *your* point of view, and only when both you and the other party appreciate and acknowledge each other's point of view can you begin to formulate a resolution that will be acceptable to both of you.

How Do I Stop Talking and Listen?

Meditate and Visualize

By *meditation*, I don't mean anything fancy. In fact, just breathing mindfully is a big help. Before I start any mediation, I have everyone take the time to sit quietly and just breathe in and breathe out. This helps cool down ill feelings so the parties don't start laying into each other from the get-go. Furthermore, I tell people

> *Most people want to respond immediately when someone says something upsetting to them.*

that when they hear something that really bothers them, they should stop and take a few deep breaths in and out before responding. This takes practice because most people want to respond immediately when someone says something upsetting. With practice, however, breathing in and out before responding gets easier. Then people have time to decide whether they really need to respond right away and, if so, how best to express their thoughts. Throughout the conversation, they can react more calmly rather than jumping in and fanning the flames of conflict.

If you're having a running argument with your neighbor about a barking dog, before you go talk to your neighbor, center and ground yourself by meditating on your breathing. Then tell yourself, "This is going to be a positive experience." I know that sounds really New Agey, but if you can approach a conflict from a more positive place, then you'll have a much better chance of actually turning it into a positive experience. The veterinarians and neighbors of barking dogs and divorcing spouses who come to me are usually thinking about all the negative things that are going to happen as soon as the other party walks through the door. By doing that, they set up the negative scenario that ends up happening. It's a self-fulfilling prophecy. I'm a firm believer that you create your own reality. Accordingly, if you think a conversation will be really difficult, it will be. However, if you approach the conversation by saying, "Hey, I know we can work this out, so I'm going to be reasonable and they're going to be reasonable," then you can help create *that* reality.

When I tell people to sit and meditate before engaging in a conversation, they think I'm crazy. However, if they visualize the conversation they want to have and how they want it to go, then when

> *I tell people to ask, "Can you tell me more?" Asking that question honestly enables people to center themselves while they're across the table from the other person.*

they engage, they don't think about yelling at the other person. Instead, they think about the conversation going great and the other person being wonderful and so forth. Because they've visualized that positive scenario in advance, it becomes easier to achieve exactly that. Before talking to someone about a conflict, spend some time visualizing how you want the conversation to go.

I also train people in techniques that allow them to reflect on the conversation while they're listening to the other party. I tell them to ask themselves, "Do I want to respond to this or let it go? Do I want to be argumentative and confrontational now? Or do I simply want to ask for more information?" I also always tell them to ask the other person, "Can you tell me more?" Asking that question honestly, without any hint of condescension, enables people to center themselves while letting the person across the table know they really want to hear them out.

Finally, after the conversation is over, reflect on how things went. This doesn't mean saying, "I should have said this! Oh man, if I just could think faster on my feet, I could have said this, and this, and this." Don't go there, because those thoughts will just perpetuate any negativity that came home with you. Instead think, "OK, this is exactly what happened. How can we use that and move forward in a positive direction?"

Use Active Listening

The best way to STOP and listen is to engage in *active listening*. That means listening to what the other party says and then repeating it back so they can understand that you are truly hearing and understanding them. It also has the immediate effect of making the other party feel that you are appreciating and acknowledging what they have to say.

If either party in a dispute has trouble with active listening, that's yet another reason to work with a mediation professional. Sometimes, if you listen to someone and then repeat what they say back to them, you can come off as condescending, without knowing it or meaning to at all. However, with a neutral mediator

> *When parties hear what they say repeated back to them, it's amazing how often they self-correct.*

there to keep the process respectful, you will hear each other clearly and be less likely to feel that you're not being taken seriously. Plus, when parties hear what they say repeated back to them, it's amazing how often they self-correct. For example, if the other party repeats back to you, "You said that I don't care about this dog," you can say, "No, you've already said you love the dog." That's self-correcting.

Recognize the Value of Taking Your Time

Recognize that you don't have to resolve the situation right away, when you're still angry. You can take your time before going to talk to your neighbor, your breeder, or your client. In fact, rushing into a conversation about a conflict may accentuate the confrontational nature of that discussion.

You might think, "I'm just putting it off, and that means I'm weak or afraid—so I'd better go over there right now because otherwise, they're going to know I'm weak and afraid!" Don't tell yourself that, and don't let anyone else tell you that, either. Instead, tell yourself, "No, waiting is not a sign of weakness. It is the ability to take time to center myself so I can visualize and create the positive conversation I want to have."

Finally, never tell yourself, "Well, it's too late now." It is never too late to have that conversation.

----

1. Yogi Berra, *The Yogi Book: I Really Didn't Say Everything I Said!* (New York: Workman, 1998), p. 42.

Chapter 5
TACTIC 2: DROP

You never really understand a person until you consider things from his point of view—until you climb into his skin and walk around in it.

—Harper Lee[1]

WHAT DOES DROP MEAN?

DROP means dropping your need to be right. Now don't worry: you *are* right—in fact, both you and the other party are right. The key here is to DROP the need to be right, because that emotional need drives the conflict and prevents it from being resolved. If you stop needing to be right and instead just listen to the other side and appreciate *their* understanding of what is

> *It's almost impossible for veterinarians to DROP the need to be right because they* are *right.*

right, then you can create a place where you are appreciating how they see the facts, not worrying about defending your idea of right against their accusations that you're wrong.

It is amazing what happens when I get opposing parties in mediations to DROP the need to be right. Once they do that, then more often than not, they realize the things they have in common outnumber the things they are at odds over. That helps them work toward a solution. But it isn't easy. In fact, it's almost impossible for veterinarians, lawyers, or almost anyone with a degree to DROP the need to be right because they *are* right—their degree and license on the wall state that these professionals know what they're talking about. It's also almost impossible for breeders to DROP because they *are* right—they've been working with this breed for thirty years, so they know all about it. And it's almost impossible for the neighbors with the barking dog to DROP because they *are* right—there's no way their dog barks for fifteen minutes straight. Finally, it's almost impossible for the person next door to the neighbor with the barking dog to DROP because they *are* right—they've been suffering from that barking for a long time.

Even though it may seem impossible to DROP, you have to do it to move forward. Fortunately, if you DROP the need to be right *right now*, that doesn't make you wrong. In mediation, both parties get to be right in their turn. So let the other person be right for the moment because as soon as they're done talking, they'll have to DROP and you'll get your chance to be right. As you let that person talk and talk and talk, just reflect back what they say, allowing them to be right and saying you can see how they feel that way. Just because you don't get to be right first doesn't mean you're wrong or any less right.

Here's the really fun part: in mediation, once a party starts talking about how right they are, they quickly run out of things to say because nobody's telling them they're wrong! If I don't tell you how wrong you are, you're not going to tell me how right you are. Instead of engaging in that endless tug-of-war, we start reflecting back and self-correcting.

In the end, as a mediator, I always find that everybody's right, because that's what I'm supposed to do. You're right, and so is he! You may say, "Are you crazy? You just told me I'm right, so how can she be right, too?" And I'll say, "Because that's how she feels, and we're going to listen to how she feels." When people start listening to how the other person feels, what comes out is "I didn't know you felt that way."

HOW DO I DROP THE NEED TO BE RIGHT?

Recognize That You Are a Professional

Even if you're a ditch digger, you'll always think you're right in any conflict involving your job. If you're a professional—especially if you're a veterinarian—your response to someone challenging your professional competence is likely "Why are you questioning me? I'm a vet—look at my degree up on the wall! Where's your degree? I'm the one who knows what he's doing here." Likewise, if you're a pet owner, you're a professional at taking care of that pet. After all, no one knows your animal better than you do. Therefore, you also believe that you're right when someone questions how you're allowing your pet to behave.

Nonetheless, your belief in your rightness means nothing to someone who is upset with you. It doesn't matter to her whether you have a degree and all kinds of awards and certifications, or if you've been a loving pet owner for decades, or whatever the case may be.

> *Recognize for yourself that you're a professional and that you don't need to feel like you have to defend your professionalism.*

The fact that a veterinarian might know tons about Lyme disease or heartworm or kennel cough means nothing to the client whose dog died. That client is heartbroken and in mourning, so if the vet tells her he's got a degree and is a professional, she'll just tell him he a professional quack. Plus, saying "I'm an expert and you're not," is a nonstarter because it just makes the other person feel too intimidated to ask questions, which is the last thing you want. It also gives the impression that you're never going to listen to them because you think they're stupid, and that's no way to resolve a conflict.

Rather than telling the other party that you're an expert, simply recognize for yourself that you're a professional and you don't need to feel like you have to defend your professionalism. If someone says you're a hack or a quack or stupid and you don't respond to that insult, that doesn't mean they're right. They said what they said, and you tell yourself that you are an expert and let it go.

Also, if you do know a lot more about the subject than the other person does, resist the urge to play the high-and-mighty keeper of secret professional knowledge. Use the same language the other party uses so you can communicate with them in a way they can easily understand. Avoid using jargon and other big words, instead drawing your vocabulary from them when you respond to their questions and present your point of view.

Be aware that treating the issue purely from a professional stance gives people the impression that you don't understand why they are upset. If you're a veterinarian, don't say or even think things like "I gave them the information in the discharge papers, so if they didn't read it, that's their problem." If you're a breeder, don't think "I told them this puppy needed a certain training regimen, and if they didn't follow it, they shouldn't be surprised the dog is out of hand." If you're a pet owner, don't think "I've explained to my neighbor that my dog is a rescue and suffered abuse early in life and that's why she's reactive. They should understand." How does that line of thinking work to resolve the conflict?

Instead, it's far better to say things like "I'm so sorry your pet isn't thriving, so let's go over the discharge papers to see if we adequately explained them to you. If we didn't explain something to you, let's do it now so we can get Fluffy to thrive." In making statements like that, you aren't countering the other party's questioning of your professional competence—you don't need to because *you* know you're the expert. You will be making the other person feel heard, understood, and respected, and you will be clearly communicating that you want to help them in a way that resolves the situation to everyone's satisfaction. That is exactly what you want to do in conflict resolution.

Use Techniques Designed to Shut Down That Voice in Your Head

When you are having a conversation, a voice in your head will say, *Don't let them say that to you! You know more than they do! Why are you letting them talk to you that way?* Don't obey that voice. It will just undermine your effort to resolve the conflict. Instead, ask yourself, "How does that voice make me feel? Do I feel better when I listen to the voice saying that the person is disrespecting me and being ridiculous and stupid? Or is that voice just making me angry and unable to listen?" Then take a breath and think, "I am hearing how this person feels about me, and I am willing to let them feel that way because that's not how I feel about myself." If you can adopt this mental stance, then you can shut down that voice in your head that doesn't make you feel good.

After you shut down the angry voice in your head, here's what you can do to keep it from coming back:

1. Visualize having a peaceful conversation.

2. Make choices that move a peaceful conversation forward.

3. View the entire conversation objectively. Look at yourself objectively and ask, "What am I doing or what am I saying to set this person off? How am I treating them?" Think about your nonverbal communication, too. Are your hands on your hips? Did you roll your eyes? Make sure you are communicating respect and a willingness to listen.

Finally, be patient with yourself. Keep in mind that DROP is the most difficult part of the program because the fact is, you know you're right. I come up against this problem all the time with my colleagues in animal law. They may be more knowledgeable and experienced than I am on some issue we're discussing. I say something and they tell me, "That's not right." I reply, "Well, it may not be right, but it's the way I feel. Since I feel this way, maybe we can have a conversation about it." Again, having a conversation that includes listening is the way to resolve disputes.

Recently, a woman said to me, "You breed dogs? Don't you know you kill dogs in shelters every time your dog has a litter?" And I said, "I know that many dogs die in shelters, but that doesn't mean that the dogs who were killed in the shelter would have been adopted by the people who bought my puppies. That's an assumption that you're willing to make but that I'm not willing to make. I believe that

> *"I am hearing how this person feels about me, and I am willing to let them feel that way because that's not how I feel about myself."*

there are people who are going to buy dogs rather than adopting them, and they should buy them from respectable breeders who know what they're doing." I stated my feelings, but I also acknowledged the assumption she was making.

Don't assume you're the only one who's right, no matter how passionately you may believe that you are. Instead, have a conversation designed to resolve the dispute. When you have that conversation, you may discover that the other party is also right—at least from their point of view.

---

1. Harper Lee, *To Kill a Mockingbird* (1960; New York: HarperCollins, 2006), p. 33.

Chapter 6

TACTIC 3: ROLL

He who angers you, conquers you.

—Elizabeth Kenny[1]

WHAT DOES ROLL MEAN?

ROLL means letting whatever someone says ROLL off your back. When someone is saying things that hurt you deeply—for example, when someone calls your professional competency into question or implies that you are a terrible person because you don't have pets— it gets your blood boiling. Naturally, you want to defend yourself.

However, you need to let the hurtful words ROLL away like rain off a duck's back. For one thing, if you don't engage, the other party will run out of things to say. Furthermore, if you just reflect what they say back and tell them, "I understand how you feel. I'm glad you told me this," when they talk to their significant other or best friend about it, they won't be able to tell the story, "Do you know what outrageous thing he said when I said this?" That's because you didn't say it. Instead, when they tell their story, the response may be "You said *what* to Dr. Smith?" or "You said *what* to our neighbor?" Because you stayed on the high ground during the conversation, the other person may come back to you and apologize. They'll at least think hard about their role in the conflict.

During a commencement address, author George Saunders asked, "Who, in your life, do you remember most fondly, with the most undeniable feelings of warmth? Those who were kindest to you, I bet."

He went on to talk about why it's often hard for us to be kind. One of the reasons is our ego-driven need for accomplishment, which can blind us to the big questions such as our connections to other people. "Still," he pointed out, "accomplishment is unreliable." He went on:

> "Succeeding," whatever that might mean to you, is hard, and the need to do so constantly renews itself (success is like a mountain that keeps growing ahead of you as you hike it), and there's the very real danger that "succeeding" will take up your whole life, while the big questions go untended.[2]

That's why when someone says something hurtful, something that disrespects your professional knowledge or diminishes you personally—something unkind—it's easy to feel attacked. Your success in your field or as a pet owner or even as a human being has just been questioned. However, it's important not to add to the unkindness. Instead, be someone people remember fondly. Take the high road and let the hurtful words ROLL off.

HOW DO I LET WHAT THE OTHER PARTY SAYS ROLL OFF MY BACK?

Ignore Criticism Without Condescending

If you say "Fine, fine, whatever you say," that will come across as condescension, which both ignores the point the other person has made while fueling their fire. Instead, you need to acknowledge the criticism respectfully. You do this by simply saying "I appreciate how you feel, and I acknowledge how you feel." If you can appreciate somebody's feelings and acknowledge their criticism respectfully, you will get much further than if you keep banging them over the head with how wrong they are.

Also, make sure to keep defensiveness in check. As anyone does, you'll want to get defensive during conflict. You'll want to think about what you're going to say rather than listening to what they're saying to you. You'll be thinking, "I want to respond now, I want to respond now …" But STOP, because engaging in that way will only fan the flames of conflict. Instead, remember that after they're done talking, it will be your turn to talk. If you haven't been going back and forth and

> *If you can acknowledge someone's criticism respectfully, you will get much further than if you keep banging them over the head with how wrong they are.*

making the conflict worse, then you'll be able to diffuse your own turmoil and respond more effectively.

There is a delicate balance to strike here. If Party A doesn't immediately respond to Party B, then Party B may say, "Are you ignoring me?" At that point, I teach people to say, "No, I am really taking in everything you have to say. I'm concerned that if I respond now, I will just fuel the fire of conflict. I need to reflect on what you've said for a little while before I respond. Is that all right with you?"

Let Them "Dump Their Bucket" So Cooler Heads Can Prevail

If you allow the other party to dump their bucket of negativity and anger and then leave and think about it, without responding in kind, they can come back and apologize if they later realize they went too far. You can also accept their apology without going *nyah, nyah*. Often upon reflection, the person will realize, "OMG, I can't believe I said that to her! And she didn't even rise to the bait—she just sat there and said she'd think about it. I'm going to go back to apologize to her." When you just let them dump their bucket and don't respond in kind, they have nothing to hold against you. This breaks up the cycle of negative tit for tat and allows for a more productive discussion to ensue.

Practice ROLLing

You can also practice letting other people's words ROLL off your back in everyday life. Regularly doing the meditation and breathing exercises we mentioned under STOP will help, and you can also try other focused relaxation exercises like tai chi and yoga. I have a colleague who worked for years as a supervisor in a customer service phone center, and part of his job was taking the complaint calls. He listened to people say nasty things about him and his company all day long. Of course,

> *If you keep the long view and wait for the client to cool down, you will be much more likely to reach a place where you're seen as the consummate professional.*

he took pride in his work and didn't like being called incompetent. However, he discovered that if he did tai chi in a conference room on his breaks, he could let all the nasty words ROLL off him. Then he could listen to the clients until they ran out of steam, understand their concerns, and propose acceptable solutions. That was a much better way to defend his professional reputation than arguing with the clients would have been.

If you keep the long view and wait for the client to cool down, you will be much more likely to reach a place where you're seen as the consummate professional whom everyone thanks for resolving the situation.

1. Elizabeth Kenny and Martha Ostenso, *And They Shall Walk* (Minneapolis–St. Paul, MN: Bruce Publishing Co., 1943), p. 13.

2. George Saunders, commencement address (Syracuse University, Syracuse, NY, May 11, 2013), **6thfloor.blogs.nytimes.com/2013/07/31/george-saunderss-advice-to-graduates/**.

Chapter 7
TACTIC 4: ADDRESS

You cannot shake hands with a clenched fist.

—Indira Gandhi[1]

WHAT DOES ADDRESS MEAN?

After all parties in the mediation STOP, DROP, and ROLL—after everyone feels heard and respected and chooses not to respond with anger—then and only then can they ADDRESS the conflict. This is where the rubber meets the road, because ADDRESSING the conflict is the only way they can KEEP their relationship. To ADDRESS the conflict is to put all the facts on the table.

HOW DO I ADDRESS THE CONFLICT?
Find a Win/Win Solution

To address the conflict, you have to want to find a win/win solution. If you're in it to win it, mediation isn't going to work.

Move Away from Avoidance, Fear, and Taking a Position

As discussed in Chapter 2, most people who are in conflict would rather avoid it. One big reason they are afraid to talk about the conflict is that they are afraid they are wrong or will be bullied about their feelings or ideas. As a self-protective measure, they take the position of "I don't care what you say—this is how it's going to be," thus avoiding talking about the conflict at all. You must move out of that corner so you can address the conflict.

Take Control of the Situation and Consider All the Options

Rather than using intercessional techniques to limit the pain of addressing the conflict—such as hiring an attorney so you don't have to talk to the other party—you can find the sweet spot for the conversation that you need to have. That's why hiring a mediator is the best approach.

Say I'm having a conflict with someone. If I talk to the other person by myself, that sweet spot may be too hard for us to find on our own. Then we may think that suffering in silence or going to litigation are our only two options. However, if we have a neutral mediator helping us, then we can find that sweet spot and come to our own resolution. Having a mediator in the room gives us the ability to take control of the situation instead of being backed into a corner by it. Then when we're in control, we can think outside the box to resolve the problem.

As a reminder, a lawyer representing you in litigation will just look at the black-and-white of win or lose. After all, when an attorney is negotiating a settlement, somebody has to win and somebody has to lose. However, if we take control of the situation, we can get into the gray area of win/win. Now we can think of solutions that a lawyer would never come up with. With all these solutions on the table, we can weigh their pros and cons and reach a balanced resolution that will work for both of us. In mediation, everyone walks away saying, "I got what I wanted and/or I settled for what I needed, and I'm happy." That's win/win.

As a mediator, how do I apply all of the above to help people address their conflict? Here's how:

Get the decision makers in the room.

First and foremost, I have to get everyone who is a decision maker in the conflict into the room together. Mediation is always about having all the decision makers in the room.

Consider a dispute between dog owners at a dog park. Such disputes are quite common, because dog parks can be like a microcosm of middle school cliques: "Oh, you have *that* kind of dog? Then you can't come in!" The disagreements that occur there are pretty unbelievable—unless you're part of one.

Let's say there's a dispute between two people whose dogs have chronically fought each other and bullied the other dogs at the park. I would have everyone from the dog park at the mediation—not just the owners of the two bullies. Alternatively, I might start with the owners of the two bullies, but eventually I would bring everybody else in so that they could have their say about the situation. That's when the conflict would really get addressed.

For example, the other people from the dog park might say, "Jane's dog is a bully, but we would never say that to Jane because Jane's a bully too." That uncovers the root of the conflict—the other dog owners are just as terrified of Jane as they are of her dog, if not more so, so they are not communicating with Jane. However, now that they're all sitting around and talking about the problem, they start to discuss what they can do to enable Jane to stay in the dog park group. Why? Because even though Jane is sometimes a bully, they actually really like her. There's a relationship worth saving. Also, people want to be fair: maybe this is the first time Jane has ever been called a bully, meaning she hasn't even known that people perceive her behavior as obnoxious. After all, even though everybody at the dog park has known all about the conflict, they hoped that if they just ignored it, it would go away. As we've seen, animal-related conflict never just goes away.

This is why I need to have all the decision makers in the conflict in the room—so that all the issues get laid out and everyone gets heard. Otherwise, the parts of the conflict involving the other dog park members will remain even after the two bullies work things out between themselves, and the conflict will just pop up again later.

What's working? What's not?

Once I've got everyone seated at the table, I bring out my big whiteboard and a bunch of sticky notes. We go through a process in which I ask them questions and they write their answers down on the sticky notes. Then I put those answers up on the board next to each other.

I start with questions like "What's working for you in this relationship? What was working for you before the incident happened? Maybe nothing, maybe a bunch of things, but what?" And then I ask, "What's not working now?" All the responses get written down and put up on the board. One party might say, "He never listened," or "He charged me too much," or "They never answered the phone when I called about the barking dogs," or "When I called, they cursed me out." Then the other party might say, "He didn't bring the dog's records from his previous vet," or "He could have just rung the doorbell and told me he had trouble with the barking dogs," or "His kids threw rocks at my house when I was at work, so I left my dogs out all day so they'd bark and scare the kids away." This is how we find out what's not working.

Solutions, solutions, and more solutions.

Then I ask, "In a perfect world, what would you like to have happen to resolve this situation?"

A pet owner in mediation with a vet might say, "I'd like to not have to pay any of the vet bills." The vet will reply, "Well, that's not going to happen because I've got to keep the lights on and pay my staff. Plus, my staff did the best they could—we all did the best we could. We wanted to help your dog, we worked hard to help him.

Plus, you gave us permission to treat him." Then the owner will retort, "My dog died, so I shouldn't have to pay anything."

I'll put a sticky note up on the board saying, "I'M NOT PAYING/I NEED TO BE PAID," and then I'll ask for more possible resolutions and put them up on the board as well. Sometimes we end up with fifty sets of resolutions up there, sometimes only ten, and sometimes just three. What's important is

> *Most of the time, we find scattered among the proposed resolutions a resolution from one side that matches a resolution from the other side.*

that we can't stop with just two, so after the first two, I prompt, "Well those are the first two proposals. What else might work?"

Next might come "HE/SHE MIGHT DROP DEAD." So I put that up there too, because you really have to acknowledge both parties' feelings. This situation is very emotional for both of them, and putting every set of proposed resolutions up on the board acknowledges everyone and every feeling involved in the conflict.

Then I keep asking each side for resolutions, respecting their feelings no matter what they are, until finally we take a step back and look at all the resolutions that have been stuck to the whiteboard. Most of the time, we find scattered among the proposed resolutions—often not proposed at the same time or on the same sticky note—a resolution from one side that matches a resolution from the other side. That's where the two sides find the common ground that allows them to resolve their dispute in a mutually satisfying way.

Questions, lots of questions.

I have a list of generic questions I use to get the discussion started in a positive direction. I also coach people to ask each other these questions to address the conflict without being confrontational. These questions fall into several categories, each of which is designed to address a different part of the conflict. The questions in the box are just examples; there is no limit to the questions one could ask in each category.

---

1. Indira Gandhi, press conference, New Delhi (October 19, 1971), quoted in Sydney H. Schanberg, "Indian and Pakistani Armies Confront Each Other Along Borders," *The New York Times* (October 20, 1971), page 6C.

QUESTIONS FOR A POSITIVE DISCUSSION

Open-Ended Questions: Used to Get the Discussion Started

- What brings you here today?
- Can you give me a little information about the disagreement?
- Can you tell me a little more about that?
- Please tell me what you are thinking/feeling?

Informational Questions: Used to Obtain Information and/or Opinions

- When did you first experience the problem with the front desk staff?
- How long have you owned your pet?
- When did you start seeing Dr. Smith to care for your pet?
- How much have you paid for veterinary services in the past year?
- How would you describe your relationship with Dr. Smith or his staff before this disagreement?

Clarifying Questions: Used to Make Abstract and General Ideas More Specific

- Can you please tell me more about why you felt that way?
- Can you please tell me how you might like to see this resolved?
- What would be the best outcome, and what would that look like to you?

Justifying Questions: Used to Explore Why a Party Holds the Position They Hold

- Can you please tell me why you feel this way?
- Can you please help me understand better how this might help you solve this disagreement?
- How do you think your adversary would respond to your offer?
- How would you respond to a similar offer?

Hypothetical Questions: Used to Carefully Introduce an Alternative View Without Forcing a Change

- Suppose you had an alternative option, one that enabled you both to win. How would that affect the disagreement and your current and future relationship?
- If you were given the opportunity to make a different choice, what would you choose to do?
- How do you think the other party might respond to an offer like this?
- Can you reflect for a moment on how that solution might look in the future?
- Can we take some time to brainstorm alternative solutions?
- Have you seen people in similar situations? What solution did they work out? How did it work for them? Would you like the same solution for you and your adversary?

Stimulating Questions: Used to Encourage New Ideas

- If the sky were the limit, could you think of a different solution?
- In what other ways might you solve this problem?
- Can we explore alternatives that are outside the box?

Participation Questions: Used to Encourage the Parties to Express Their Needs, Desires, and Wants

- What do you think about that?
- Tell me what you think about that suggested solution?
- How do you feel about the suggested solution?

Focusing Questions: Used to Help the Parties Return to the Core Issues

- Can we talk about where you think we can go from here?
- How do you see this relating to the issue before us?
- Can we take one issue at a time?

Comparison Questions: Used to Compare All the Options Suggested

- Can we look at all the options without comment first?
- Which of the options suggested have common outcomes?
- Looking at all the options, how would you rank them from best to worst?
- Do any two of the suggested solutions work well for you?

Closure Questions: Used to Encourage and Support Decision Making

- Would you like to take time to think about this suggested solution?
- Would having more time to decide make it easier to evaluate the solution?
- Have we come to agreement on that issue?
- Let me ask you both, have we spent enough time on that issue?
- Are you ready for us to move on?

Evaluation Questions: Used as Reality Checks to Help Parties Assess and Acknowledge Their Progress

- Can we take a moment to see what we have in common?
- Can we take time to evaluate our differences?
- Why do you think you may be blocked on this issue?
- What might happen if you tried this suggested solution?

Chapter 8
TACTIC 5: KEEP

My interest is in the future because I'm going to be spending the rest of my life there.

—Charles F. Kettering[1]

WHAT DOES KEEP MEAN?

ADDRESSING the conflict means people get to KEEP their relationship. In fact, mediation relies on the parties choosing to KEEP their relationship because only then are they motivated to ADDRESS the conflict. As mentioned before, people often want to KEEP their relationship without even knowing that's what they want. People who have been friends for twenty years may swear up and down that they never want to speak to each other again—but after they've gone through mediation, heard each other out, and respected each other's feelings, they often decide they want to give their friendship another chance. This often also allows them to KEEP their relationship with an animal they both care about. These relationships make the future brighter. That's the opportunity that mediation offers and what the mediator encourages.

HOW DO I KEEP THE RELATIONSHIP?

Use Evaluative Skills

Ask yourself how important it is to you to KEEP this relationship. For example, how important is it that you can wave to your neighbor when you drive by? If that's not important to you, then you're not highly motivated to resolve the conflict. If it is important, however, then you're open to doing what's necessary to resolve the conflict via a win/win solution.

Is the relationship business or personal? You might feel more motivated to maintain a business relationship than a personal one, or vice versa, so again, consider the nature of the relationship and how strongly you feel about it.

What's the impact on other people if the relationship falls apart? How uncomfortable will other people at the dog park or canine agility class be if you and the owner of that other dog aren't speaking to each other? What about the other people in your apartment complex when you and the couple in 221B are threatening to sue each other and trying to rope in other residents as potential witnesses? These are innocent bystanders, and their lives would be more pleasant if you and the other party could speak civilly. Maybe that's not very important to you, or maybe it is.

> *You might extend yourself to keep a business relationship but not a personal relationship, or vice versa.*

Finally, what's the potential impact on your pet, if it's your pet involved? Say you're getting a divorce and for all kinds of reasons, you really don't want to have anything more to do with your ex. You're even angrier when your ex is awarded custody of the cats. But what if down the road one of the cats needs long-term care for a chronic illness? Maybe your ex won't have the time or the money to help that cat maintain its quality of life, or maybe they just won't want to make the effort. If the two of you aren't talking, you might not even know about the situation. However, if the two of you do have a way to communicate, at least about the cats, then you will know the cat is sick and maybe your former spouse will even let you help. That would be in the best interest of the cat. Maintaining the relationship with your cats may not be worth the cost of having contact with your ex, or maybe it is worth it.

Bottom line: Only you can decide whether KEEPING the relationship makes sense.

The Sooner, the Better

If you wait until the conflict is way out of control, you and the other party will be angrier, your relationship more tenuous, and your desire to KEEP the relationship weaker. That's why it's better to address a conflict early. Another reason is that the other person may not even know they're upsetting you. It's better to tell them sooner what's upsetting you and what they should do about it than to wait in silence for a month and then come down on them like a ton of bricks (remember "suffering in silence" and "explosive confrontation" from Chapter 2?). By approaching them right away, you can get the problem fixed sooner and with less drama.

This is where conflict coaching can come in to rescue a relationship. The conflict coach can help you deal with people in a way that prevents continued conflict or nips it in the bud, before you even get to the point of needing mediation.

----

1. Charles F. Kettering, "Thoughts on the Business of Life," *Forbes* (1948).

Chapter 9

TACTIC 6: ACKNOWLEDGE AND APPRECIATE

Resolving conflict is rarely about who is right. It is about acknowledgment and appreciation of differences.

—Thomas F. Crum[1]

WHAT DO ACKNOWLEDGE AND APPRECIATE MEAN?

You need to ACKNOWLEDGE the other person is sharing their point of view, and you need to APPRECIATE the fact that they're doing it. Note that APPRECIATING is different from ACKNOWL-EDGING. ACKNOWLEDGING means you are in the room, you are present, you are facilitating the conversation along with the mediator and the other party, and you are engaging with the other party in an effort to find a resolution. APPRE-CIATING is placing value on the fact that another party has

> *APPRECIATING the fact that someone is sharing their own ideas about the conflict and how to resolve it does not mean you're agreeing with them.*

shared their point of view with you. It doesn't mean you're agreeing with them—it just means you're APPRECIATING the fact that they are sharing their own ideas about the conflict and how to resolve it.

HOW DO I ACKNOWLEDGE AND APPRECIATE?

Reflect the Other Person's Words Back to Them

If you reflect back to people what they say when they are angry—not with a condescending tone but just exactly what they say—there are several things that could happen. They may feel heard, understood, respected, and appreciated. They may self-correct because they re- alize how harsh they sound and they don't mean to come across like that. Or they may set you straight because you didn't hear them correctly. The mediator will reflect what both parties are saying so they can hear it out of the mediator's mouth as well.

Role-play in Advance

During conflict coaching or in preparation for mediation, I sit down with a client and role-play how the conversation with the other par- ty might go. In the process, I help clients to recognize their own voice and hear things the other party will say that need to be AC- KNOWLEDGED and APPRECIATED.

Get Feedback from an Observer

In my conflict resolution workshops, I have participants break up into groups and engage in mock mediations. One person plays the mediator, two other group members play the people in conflict, and yet another func- tions as a neutral ob- server. The observer often notices a lot of verbal and nonverbal

> *An observer can offer a huge insight that gets the person thinking about how they're coming across and helps them become less confrontational.*

communication that the people engaged in the conflict are completely unconscious of. The feedback gained through this exercise can be very valuable.

For example, if someone in a mock mediation exercise thought he had said nothing confrontational during the session, he might ask the observer for feedback and be surprised when the observer says, "That thing you said really pissed me off, and I'm not even the one you said it to." That can be huge insight that gets the person thinking about how he's coming across and helps him adjust his use of language to become less confrontational.

Understand the Costs and Benefits of Valuing APPRECIATION and ACKNOWLEDGMENT

If you ACKNOWLEDGE and APPRECIATE someone, they will feel that you're listening to them and giving them the respect they deserve. The cost of not doing so is that you will lose the friendship, lose the business, lose the relationship with your pet, or whatever it is that's worth keeping.

For example, if you're a veterinarian and you value the relationship with your clients—and all the prospective clients they might talk to in person or online—then the cost of not talking to them and not listening to them is losing those current and future relationships. If you do not want to pay that cost, then you must ACKNOWLEDGE and APPRECIATE your client in a way that allows you to ADDRESS and resolve the conflict.

Realize That the Primary Goal Is Understanding, Not Agreement

Agreement is never what I go into a discussion looking for. Instead, the goal is for you to better understand me and for me to better understand you. If we can come to an agreement, that's great, but if not, at least I'll know how you feel and you'll know how I feel. Therefore, engage with the other person in the belief that reaching an agreement is secondary to finding out how that person feels and APPRECIATING their feelings. In fact, going through the process of understanding and APPRECIATING each other starts to defuse the conflict. It allows both of you to be right even though you have different points of view. Even further, it helps you start to find that gray area where you can become creative in resolving your dispute via a win/win solution.

Also, while there may be great value in agreeing, there may be costs involved, too. For example, in a divorce, you may want to keep your relationship with the dog but never see your ex again. The cost of reaching an agreement might be having to see your ex every time you see your dog.

> *If we can come to an agreement, that's great, but if not, at least I'll know how you feel and you'll know how I feel.*

If you can't bear to pay that cost, you may instead have to pay the cost of hiring someone to transport the dog from your ex's house to your house on a regular basis. If you and your ex will pay for this transportation, you'll both have to decide whether that's a cost you're willing to bear so the dog stay in both your lives. It's possible that you both decide that the cost of seeing each other once a month while you hand off the dog is less "expensive" than the alternative. Or perhaps you're not willing to pay either of these costs to KEEP your relationship with the dog. Figuring this out is part of the process of finding the sweet spot.

Therefore, you may not want to make coming to an agreement paramount until you can work out the costs and benefits of any such agreement. If you only see costs in making an agreement, agreeing won't be much of a priority. Alternatively, if you enter into a discussion feeling that you have to come to an agreement or bust, then the process may quickly become demoralizing when it doesn't seem to be leading to agreement. Finally, you may be so wedded to a particular position that agreement on anything but what you want will be impossible. If, on the other hand, you go in with the simple belief that it is beneficial to have a conversation so you can understand the other person better, without the idea that you have to come to an agreement, then you can often reach a better place from which to construct an agreement that truly satisfies all parties.

> *If you go in with the belief that it is beneficial to have a conversation so you can understand the other party better, then you can often reach a better place from which to make an agreement.*

1. Thomas F. Crum, *The Magic of Conflict: Turning a Life of Work into a Work of Art* (New York: Simon and Schuster, 1987), p. 49.

Chapter 10
PUTTING IT ALL TOGETHER

I find the great thing in this world is not so much where we stand, as in what direction we are moving.

—Oliver Wendell Holmes Sr.[1]

Mediation works because when you STOP, DROP, and ROLL, you put out the flames of conflict. If you STOP talking and just listen, DROP the need to be right, and let what the other party says ROLL off your back, then the fire of emotional conflict cannot burn you, nor can it be fed by the fuel of anger and disagreement. Using STOP, DROP, and ROLL enables anyone who has a pet, takes care of people's pets for a living, or lives near other people's pets to have conversations that are less confrontational, more constructive, and more likely to lead to peaceful resolutions. Employing STOP, DROP, and ROLL also enables pet owners to hear what their veterinarian, ex-spouse, or neighbors have to say without taking it as an attack.

Then, once the parties have used STOP, DROP, and ROLL so that they all feel heard and respected by each other, they are able to ADDRESS their conflict, getting all the facts out on the table and all their proposed solutions up on the board. Using the techniques described in this book, the parties and their mediator can look at the conflict objectively, understanding what's at the root of it and which solutions would be acceptable to everyone.

Driving all of this is a desire among the parties to KEEP their relationship, even if they don't realize it at the time. To allow all that to happen, the parties must ACKNOWLEDGE and APPRECIATE each other, realizing that the energy they're expending to simply understand each other is a worthy effort all by itself that should be honored.

If the people involved do all of this, they will be able to resolve their conflict and retain their relationship at an affordable price—the exact opposite of what would have happened if they had gone to litigation.

---

1. Oliver Wendell Holmes Sr., *The Autocrat of the Breakfast Table* (1858; Boston: James R. Osgood and Co., 1873), p. 68, **www.gutenberg.org/ebooks/751**.

Self-Assessment 2
A MEDITATION ON MEDIATION

Think about the six tactics discussed in Section Two:

STOP talking and listen	**ADDRESS** the conflict
DROP the need to be right	**KEEP** the relationship
Let what the other party says **ROLL** off your back	**ACKNOWLEDGE** and **APPRECIATE** the other party

Draw a circle around the one that resonates the most for you. Describe below what makes it meaningful.

_____

_____

_____

_____

Now draw a box around the tactic that may be the most difficult for you. Describe below why you think it will be challenging.

_____

_____

_____

_____

(continued)

Have your ideas about mediation changed after reading Section Two of this book? If so, how?

_____

_____

_____

_____

Think about a conflict you are having now or one in the recent past. How could mediation make a difference (or have made a difference) in the outcome?

_____

_____

_____

_____

What questions do you still have about mediation?

_____

_____

_____

_____

Section Three
GET STARTED

The hardest step is over the threshold.

—Chinese proverb

You are ready to stop, drop, and roll and to address the conflict, keep the relationship, and acknowledge and appreciate the other person or people involved. Whether you picked up this book because you're in a conflict now and want a solution, or whether you know a conflict could arise someday and just want to be prepared, you need to know how to find expert assistance to help you use the techniques outlined in these pages. The following chapter gives you some useful advice for taking that step.

Chapter 11
HOW TO CHOOSE A MEDIATOR OR CONFLICT COACH

The greatest trust between man and man is the trust of giving counsel.

—Francis Bacon[1]

So now that you know mediation is the way to go when you get into a dispute with someone over an animal, what's the best way to find a mediator? Well, that depends on many things: your location, your objectives, and whether cost is a factor. Moreover, finding a mediator who will handle an animal-related dispute can sometimes be a challenge.

> *Finding a mediator who will handle an animal-related dispute can sometimes be a challenge.*

There's a simple reason for this: mediators know how emotional animal-related disputes are, so some mediators don't want to handle that kind of drama and will simply avoid taking animal-related cases.

But the good news is that Google is your friend. With some basic knowledge in hand, you can do a lot of up-front research on the Web to become familiar with the mediators and mediation services in your area. Using the guidelines below, take your time researching your options before making contact with a mediator to find out if he or she is the right person to help you address your conflict.

WEB SEARCHES

Start by doing an Internet search on "mediators," followed by your ZIP code. This will bring up the websites of professional mediators in your area. Study each website to see if the mediator has experience in animal-related conflict resolution. Research several mediators before making contact with any of them and make sure to talk with at least a few before choosing one.

If through a simple search you don't find a selection of mediators who are qualified to handle animal-related conflicts, visit the websites of the following organizations to find mediators in your area.

Mediators + More. I am pleased to be a member of this organization comprised of about a dozen distinguished lawyers from varied practice areas now also serving as experienced mediators. We apply the in-depth, substantive knowledge we have acquired in our various practices to help parties resolve disputes without costly, destructive litigation. Mediators + More was formed to address concerns about generalist mediators' all too frequent lack of familiarity with the subject matter of a particular dispute. The organization is based in New York but has a national and international reach. See **mediatorsplusmore.com**.

Mediation.org. This is a professional association for mediators, established by the American Arbitration Association (AAA). As mentioned, arbitration is not mediation, so AAA has set up Mediation.org as a separate network for mediators and individuals seeking to hire mediators. The website's "Find a Mediator" service (**mediation.org/mediation/faces/find_a_mediator**) allows individuals to search for local mediators and view their résumés and qualifications online. However, please note that Mediate.org makes no representation as to the accuracy of the information mediators post about themselves on the "Find a Mediator" service.

On the other hand, Mediate.org does provide training and certification for mediators, so you can check whether mediators in your local area are certified. In addition, Mediate.org has staff mediators who do online mediation for simple disputes. In online mediation, two disputing parties can meet via the Web instead of face-to-face and have their mediation facilitated from start to finish by an AAA staff mediator. The parties communicate with the mediator and each other via a chat room and instant messaging, and a flat fee pays for the entire process (see **mediation.org/mediation/ faces/mediation_services/online_mediation**). However, be aware that since Mediate.org specifies that online mediation should only be used for fairly straightforward mediations, it might not be the best option for an animal-related mediation, given all the deep-running emotions involved. The lack of face-to-face communication and the other limitations of online communication may rob mediation participants of the ability to feel fully heard, understood, and appreciated on both the intellectual and emotional level.

Mediate.com. This website is a leading provider of online services for mediators. It is mainly geared toward mediators themselves—providing them with information, support, and training—but it has an extensive directory that individuals can use to find mediators in their local area. See **mediate.com/mediator/search.cfm**.

CIVIL COURTS AND MEDIATION CENTERS

If you're unable to find a suitable mediator in your area through searching the Web, then call or visit your local courthouse and ask for recommendations of local mediators who handle disputes involving animals. The civil courts often use mediators to settle disputes, and even criminal courts send low-level cases to mediation when all parties would be better served through alternative dispute resolution. Some court systems have their own websites and list their associated mediators online, but talking to an individual at the courthouse (if available) might better help you find a mediator who is experienced in disputes involving animals.

In addition, there are community mediation centers and programs in almost every state. These mediation services are usually provided for free, so they're a good option for people seeking to keep costs as low as possible. To find community mediation centers in your area, check the website of the National Association for Community Mediation (**nafcm.org**) or just google "community mediation" followed by your ZIP code to locate the closest community mediation center. However, before using your local community mediation services, inquire as to whether the volunteer mediators working there have experience in resolving animal-related disputes. It's important to emphasize this because, as mentioned, the highly emotional nature of animal-related disputes can be overwhelming to some less experienced mediators.

LAW SCHOOL ALTERNATIVE DISPUTE RESOLUTION (ADR) PROGRAMS

Many law schools have training programs in alternative dispute resolution (ADR), and hands-on mediation of actual disputes between individuals is a key part of such programs. To support these efforts, the law schools run outreach programs that bring individuals together with student mediators who provide ADR services for a fee, usually on a sliding scale. Using a student mediator can be cost-effective, but it's unlikely that a student mediator will have experience in mediating disputes involving animals. Therefore, it's essential that you inquire whether the student mediators available from a law school ADR program have experience mediating animal-related disputes.

To find a law school ADR program in your area, check the Mediate.com links to law school programs at **mediate.com/articles/lawadrprogramlinks.cfm**.

OTHER PROFESSIONAL ASSOCIATIONS AND NONPROFIT ORGANIZATIONS

Finally, there are many other professional associations for mediators and many nonprofits that support and promote mediation at the state and local level and worldwide. For example, I am a member of the Family and Divorce Mediation Council, the New York Association of Collaborative Professionals, and the International Academy of Collaborative Professionals. All such organizations can serve as information resources to help individuals contact experienced mediators. Here is a list of websites with links to many of these organizations:

Association for Conflict Resolution:
imis100us2.com/acr/acr/default.aspx

Association of Attorney-Mediators: **attorney-mediators.org**

HG.org's list of arbitration and media associations in the United States:
hg.org/arbitration-mediation-associations-usa.html

Mediate.com's listing of nonprofit organizations that support mediation: **mediate.com/organizations/**

National Association of Certified Mediators:
mediatorcertification.org

---

1. Francis Bacon, "Of Counsel," in *Essays, Civil and Moral*, vol. 3, pt. 1. (New York: P. F. Collier & Son, 1909–1914), **www.bartleby.com/3/1/20.html**.

Conclusion

In America today, we are living at a time of nearly unprecedented political polarization. This didn't come out of nowhere—it's been building for quite a while. In the 1990s, we saw the first presidential impeachment in over a century, and then the disputed election of 2000 and the controversial wars after 9/11 made it even harder for people on different sides of the aisle to reach out and have a dialogue. The terminology of "red states" and "blue states" entered our national lexicon, suggesting that we are a nation of two peoples rather than one. Then in 2008, some thought the election of our first African American president might usher in a postracial age of renewed understanding, but instead it brought to the surface sharper divisions than ever. Since then, we've found new conflicts to divide us, and that led the *Washington Post* to report on some depressing research:

> Up until the mid-1980s, the typical American held the view that partisans on the other side operated with good intentions. But that has changed in dramatic fashion, as a study published last year by Stanford and Princeton researchers demonstrates.
>
> It has long been agreed that race is the deepest divide in American society. But that is no longer true.… [The study states that] "the level of partisan animus in the American public exceeds racial hostility."
>
> … Also of note is that the partisan polarization occurs even though Americans aren't all that split on

policies or ideology. Their partisanship is more tribal than anything—the result of an ill-informed electorate. [One researcher notes,] "In order to have an understanding of the ideology of your party and the opposing party you have to have a lot of information," and "that's something that just doesn't happen for the majority of the electorate.... However, most people understand their side is good and the opposing side is bad, so it's much easier for them to form these emotional opinions of political parties."[1]

In other words, we have decided that demonizing the other party is easier than trying to understand them. As a result, we've sacrificed our relationship with Americans of different political persuasions because we don't think that keeping our relationship with them is worth the effort of addressing our conflict with them. We just don't bother to try to understand them and come to some sort of agreement—even if it's just agreeing to disagree. We may see this kind of conflict avoidance as the easy way out, but look what it has gotten us: a divided and dysfunctional government in Washington and a divided population that grows more willfully ignorant of each other by the year. This same kind of evaluation of each other's position occurs in conflicts over animals, whether it's the family pet or a circus elephant.

Is this what we want? Or is there a better way?

Instead of talking past each other, we need to start sitting down with each other across a table and take turns just listening to each other. We need to quit it with the flame wars on Facebook and find a way to re-engage with each other, in person and with respect. We need to stop focusing on what Freud called the "narcissism of small differences"—hating people with whom we have a lot in common but who disagree with us on just a few things. We are all people after all, and if we take the time to hear each other out and feel respected and acknowledged by each other, we can find win/win solutions to our problems that don't involve anyone getting their pound of flesh. While we won't all get everything we want, we can at least start to repair vital relationships upon which America was founded: *E Pluribus Unum*—Out of Many, One.

The mediation and conflict-coaching techniques I've described in this book give us one way to start down that road, at least as individuals. Most important, our beloved animals don't have to suffer when we humans have disagreements. I hope you'll consider using these strategies to address the conflicts in your own life in general and over an animal. They can help you keep and repair your own relationships. In conflicts involving animals, *please* always call a local mediation professional before calling a litigator. Litigation is the last thing you want to do when your beloved pet or an animal in need is at the center of a dispute, while mediation is the best way to resolve a dispute in a way that puts the welfare of the animal first. Who knows? It might even make you some new friends along the way—something a dog would surely approve of.

1. Dana Milbank, "America's New Cycle of Partisan Hatred," *The Washington Post*, April 17, 2015, **www.washingtonpost.com/opinions/americas-new-tribal-cycle-of-hatred/2015/04/17/67794040-e50a-11e4-905f-cc896d379a32_story.html**, quoting from Shanto Iyengar and Sean J. Westwood, *Fear and Loathing Across Party Lines: New Evidence on Group Polarization*, **pcl.stanford.edu/research/2014/iyengar-ajps-group-polarization.pdf**.

ABOUT THE AUTHOR

DEBRA A. VEY VODA-HAMILTON spent 30 years as a practicing litigator, but she is now a full-time mediator and conflict coach for people in disputes over animals. She works both nationwide and internationally. She has far-reaching experience in resolving interpersonal conflicts involving animals, and she is also well-known in the world of purebred dogs as a top breeder and exhibitor of Irish setters and long-haired dachshunds.

Debra speaks widely on the topic of how mediation techniques can help people address conflicts without litigation. She has presented at veterinary schools, the American Kennel Club, the American Veterinary Medical Law Association, the Society of Animal Welfare Administrators, the Living With Animals conference, state bar association Animal Law Committee meetings, and animal interest group meetings. Debra also writes a blog for Hamilton Law and Mediation and is a contributor to the Solo Practice University blog and the *Canine Chronicle*. She has been featured in *Forbes*, the *Wall Street Journal*, *US News and World Report*, and the *New York Times*.

As the principal at Hamilton Law and Mediation, PLLC—the nation's first solo mediation practice dedicated to helping people resolve conflicts over animals—Debra uses alternative dispute resolution to help address disagreements over the family pet during divorce, neighbors' arguments over a barking dog, and confrontations between clients and veterinarians and other professionals who work with animals. HLM also looks forward to helping animal rights and welfare advocates see the benefit of having a conversation about the best interests of all parties—especially the animals—to resolve animal-related disputes.

Debra is admitted to practice law in all New York State courts. She is certified as a mediator and collaborative professional and has worked with various court-based mediation programs in New York City (Queens-Community Mediation Service) and in Westchester and Rockland Counties in New York (Westchester and Rockland Mediation Centers).

Made in the USA
Columbia, SC
03 September 2021